Bipolar
Disorder

Diseases and Disorders

ReferencePoint
Press®

San Diego, CA

**Other books in the Compact Research
Diseases and Disorders set:**

*For a complete list of titles please visit www.referencepointpress.com.

Bipolar Disorder

Peggy J. Parks

Diseases and Disorders

ReferencePoint Press®

San Diego, CA

© 2015 ReferencePoint Press, Inc.
Printed in the United States

For more information, contact:
ReferencePoint Press, Inc.
PO Box 27779
San Diego, CA 92198
www.ReferencePointPress.com

Picture credits:
Cover: Dreamstime and iStockphoto.com
Maury Aaseng: 33–34, 47–49, 61-62, 75–77
Science Photo Library: 19
Thinkstock Images: 13

LIBRARY OF CONGRESS CATALOGING-IN-PUBLICATION DATA

Parks, Peggy J., 1951–
    Bipolar disorder / by Peggy J. Parks.
        pages cm. -- (Compact research series)
    Includes bibliographical references and index.
    ISBN-13: 978-1-60152-640-3 (hardback)
    ISBN-10: 1-60152-640-7 (hardback)
    1. Manic-depressive illness--Juvenile literature. I. Title.
    RC516.P36   2014
    616.89'5--dc23
                                                          2013040172

Contents

Foreword

66Where is the knowledge we have lost in information?99

—T.S. Eliot, "The Rock."

As modern civilization continues to evolve, its ability to create, store, distribute, and access information expands exponentially. The explosion of information from all media continues to increase at a phenomenal rate. By 2020 some experts predict the worldwide information base will double every seventy-three days. While access to diverse sources of information and perspectives is paramount to any democratic society, information alone cannot help people gain knowledge and understanding. Information must be organized and presented clearly and succinctly in order to be understood. The challenge in the digital age becomes not the creation of information, but how best to sort, organize, enhance, and present information.

ReferencePoint Press developed the *Compact Research* series with this challenge of the information age in mind. More than any other subject area today, researching current issues can yield vast, diverse, and unqualified information that can be intimidating and overwhelming for even the most advanced and motivated researcher. The *Compact Research* series offers a compact, relevant, intelligent, and conveniently organized collection of information covering a variety of current topics ranging from illegal immigration and deforestation to diseases such as anorexia and meningitis.

The series focuses on three types of information: objective single-author narratives, opinion-based primary source quotations, and facts and statistics. The clearly written objective narratives provide context and reliable background information. Primary source quotes are carefully selected and cited, exposing the reader to differing points of view, and facts and statistics sections aid the reader in evaluating perspectives. Presenting these key types of information creates a richer, more balanced learning experience.

For better understanding and convenience, the series enhances information by organizing it into narrower topics and adding design features that make it easy for a reader to identify desired content. For example, in *Compact Research: Illegal Immigration*, a chapter covering the economic impact of illegal immigration has an objective narrative explaining the various ways the economy is impacted, a balanced section of numerous primary source quotes on the topic, followed by facts and full-color illustrations to encourage evaluation of contrasting perspectives.

The ancient Roman philosopher Lucius Annaeus Seneca wrote, "It is quality rather than quantity that matters." More than just a collection of content, the *Compact Research* series is simply committed to creating, finding, organizing, and presenting the most relevant and appropriate amount of information on a current topic in a user-friendly style that invites, intrigues, and fosters understanding.

Bipolar Disorder at a Glance

Bipolar Disorder Defined

Bipolar disorder is a serious, often debilitating mental illness that was formerly called manic depression.

Symptoms

Bipolar disorder is characterized by two drastically different kinds of mood swings: the lows of depression and the extreme highs known as mania.

Types

The two main types of bipolar disorder are bipolar I and bipolar II. A third type, known as cyclothymic disorder, is a milder form of bipolar disorder.

Prevalence

Health officials estimate lifetime prevalence of bipolar disorder in the United States to be 3.9 percent of the population.

Causes

Scientists do not know what causes bipolar disorder, but they believe it develops due to a complex interaction of biological and environmental factors.

Triggers

Stress and many types of life events can trigger manic or depressive episodes in someone who is biologically vulnerable to developing bipolar disorder.

Associated Problems

Bipolar disorder can have a negative effect on a person's quality of life, which can lead to problems such as substance abuse and a high suicide risk.

Diagnosis

No test can diagnose bipolar disorder, so physicians rely on medical history, an evaluation of the patient's symptoms, and criteria for the illness established by the American Psychiatric Association.

Treatment Regimens

Most people with bipolar disorder are treated with several types of medications combined with psychotherapy.

Overcoming Bipolar Disorder

Bipolar disorder is a chronic illness, meaning one that is lifelong. With the right treatment, many sufferers are able to keep their symptoms under control and live happy, productive lives.

Overview

❝Bipolar Disorder is one of the most severe mental disorders a person could have.❞

—Seth Meyers, a clinical psychologist with the Los Angeles County Department of Mental Health.

❝When you have bipolar disorder, your brain's accelerator is stuck. At full speed, it launches you into a manic episode. In low gear, it grinds you down into a deep depression.❞

—Candida Fink, a New York City psychiatrist and the author of *Bipolar Disorder for Dummies*, and Joe Kraynak, the book's coauthor.

Actress Carrie Fisher, whose name is well known to *Star Wars* fans, is very familiar with the extreme highs and lows of bipolar disorder. Diagnosed in her twenties, Fisher's moods alternate between lasting bouts of intense excitability (known as mania) and periods of crushing depression. For years she kept her symptoms under control by adhering to a strict treatment regimen. But in February 2013, when Fisher was scheduled to perform as the headliner on a Caribbean cruise, her mania flared up and spiraled out of control. "I went completely off the rails,"[1] she says.

A Night Worth Forgetting

The warning signs began to appear shortly after Fisher boarded the ship. She was unable to respond when her assistant talked to her. She had a bizarre, frantic need to grab a pen and write on every available surface, from the inside of books to walls and the floor. At night she lay awake with her eyes wide open despite taking excessive doses of a prescription drug that usually helped her sleep. "I've never taken that many in my life,"[2] she says. By the time Fisher was scheduled to perform, she was in the throes of a full-blown manic episode.

Once onstage, she tried to sing but could not remember the song lyrics. While attempting to interact with the audience, she rambled on, slurring her words and causing people to mistakenly assume that she was drunk. Yet Fisher has no memory of this and only knows what happened because of what she was told afterward. "I don't really remember what I did," she says. "I know it got bad. I was in a very severe manic state, which bordered on psychosis. . . . I wasn't clear on what was going on. I was just trying to survive."[3] Seeing that she was in trouble, several people went onstage and helped her back to her room. The next day Fisher left the ship and flew to Los Angeles, California, where she checked into a psychiatric hospital for treatment. She then moved to a residential facility, where she could stay while becoming accustomed to new medications.

> " Bipolar I is considered the most severe form of bipolar disorder, largely because of how intense and incapacitating the mania can be. "

What Is Bipolar Disorder?

Formerly known as manic-depressive illness (or manic depression), bipolar disorder is a serious, often debilitating mental illness. Its defining characteristic is the coupling of two extremes: manic episodes that alternate with bouts of depression. Although some mental health professionals still prefer to use the former name (and continue to do so), the American Psychiatric Association (APA) officially changed it to bipolar disorder in 1980. In his book *The Bipolar Disorder Survival Guide*, psychologist David J. Miklowitz explains the reasoning behind the name: "It is called *bipolar* because the mood swings occur between two poles, high and low, as opposed to unipolar disorder [major depression], where mood swings occur along only one pole—the lows."[4]

Miklowitz's use of the term *mood swings* is common among mental health professionals when describing bipolar disorder's highs and lows—but this should not be confused with normal moodiness. The variations in mood experienced by people with bipolar disorder are severe and long lasting. The American Academy of Child & Adolescent Psychiatry explains: "While everyone has good and bad moods, the unprovoked and intense highs and lows of people with bipolar disorder can be unpredictable, extreme, and debilitating."[5] These mood episodes do not follow a predictable, set pattern, meaning that depression does not always follow mania and vice versa.

Bipolar I and II

A detailed description of bipolar disorder is found in the APA's *Diagnostic and Statistical Manual of Mental Disorders* (*DSM*), which is often referred to as the psychiatrist's bible. The *DSM* has been published since 1952, when the inaugural edition included a category called "manic-depressive reactions." It has been revised a number of times over the years, with the newest version (the *DSM-5*) released in May 2013. The book now contains a category called "bipolar and related disorders," which lists three main types: bipolar I, bipolar II, and cyclothymic disorder. Several other classifications also appear in the 2013 *DSM*, such as "bipolar disorder not elsewhere classified." This is used with patients who have bipolar disorder symptoms but whose condition does not fit the criteria for any of the defined types.

> **Throughout the world, males and females of all races, ethnicities, and walks of life are affected by bipolar disorder.**

Bipolar I is considered the most severe form of bipolar disorder, largely because of how intense and incapacitating the mania can be. To be classified as bipolar I, an individual must have had at least one manic episode, accompanied by a marked change in energy, at some point during his or her lifetime. The mania must have lasted a week or longer or been severe enough that the person needed to be hospitalized. Most people with bipolar I also suffer from depressive episodes, but the primary symptom is mania. "If you have had a manic

Bipolar disorder is characterized by unpredictable and intense highs and lows. Stressful life events can trigger the heightened emotional state and deep depression experienced by someone with bipolar disorder.

episode but no depressions," says Miklowitz, "your doctor will still diagnose you with bipolar I disorder. This is because he or she assumes that a depression will eventually occur if the disorder is not treated adequately."[6]

Bipolar II is similar in many ways to bipolar I, but it involves a condition known as hypomania rather than mania. Therese J. Borchard, a writer and editor who has bipolar II, describes hypomania as a mild to moderate level of mania that is "generally a less destructive state than mania." Borchard goes on to say that some people with bipolar II embrace their hypomania, as she explains: "It may feel good to the person who experiences it and may even be associated with good functioning and enhanced productivity. Therefore, even when family and friends learn to recognize the mood swings as possible bipolar disorder, the person may deny that anything is wrong." This can lead to serious problems, however, as Borchard explains: "Without proper treatment . . . hypomania can turn into severe mania in some people or can switch into depression."[7]

When people with bipolar II do "switch into depression," it can be a dreadful experience. Whereas the primary (and most severe) characteristic of bipolar I is mania, depressive episodes are often the biggest problem for bipolar II sufferers. One reason is that their bouts with depression last longer, as Charlottesville, Virginia, psychologist Russ Federman explains: "For many people with BP II, far more time is spent in depression than when compared to those with BP I." Describing depression as a "blah, pleasureless, low-energy, miserable, unhappy experience," Federman says that it can be more difficult for people with bipolar II to endure because it is a chronic condition, meaning ongoing and long lasting. He writes: "It's one thing to say—'Here I am stuck in a depressive funk.' But there's a more potent downward pull when the individual is thinking—'Here I am stuck in my bipolar depression for the sixth time!'"[8]

> " Even experts who are convinced of the link between biological factors and bipolar disorder recognize the likelihood that other factors are involved as well. "

Cyclothymia

Cyclothymic disorder, also called cyclothymia, is generally described as a milder form of bipolar disorder. People with cyclothymia alternate between hypomania and bouts of depression, with multiple episodes that last for two years or more. These episodes can cause problems for the individual but are not severe enough to be classified as bipolar disorder. In their book *Bipolar Disorder for Dummies*, psychiatrist Candida Fink and coauthor Joe Kraynak refer to cyclothymia as "bipolar lite," saying that it is a "muted form of bipolar that nevertheless interferes with a person's life."[9]

A young woman from the United Kingdom named Lizzie was diagnosed with cyclothymia in 2013. Because she had never heard of the illness, she began doing some Internet research—and was dismayed to find it repeatedly described as "mild." She writes: "Again and again, in page after page the same word kept cropping up; 'mild.' 'Mild' was like a kick in the teeth to me."[10] As she continued hunting for information, Lizzie began to feel encouraged by what she read on some online communities of people with cyclothymia. "They were telling each other something important," she says. "Cyclothymia isn't mild, it is a milder manifestation of bipolar symptoms. Bipolar is to cyclothymia as a rock shattered in a massive earthquake is to a rock worn down to dust by steady, reliable, constant erosion; either way it gets worn away."[11]

Who Develops Bipolar Disorder?

Throughout the world, males and females of all races, ethnicities, and walks of life are affected by bipolar disorder. A 2011 study led by National Institute of Mental Health (NIMH) researcher Kathleen R. Merikangas found that worldwide prevalence of the illness is approximately 2.4 percent. According to the NIMH, lifetime prevalence in the United States is 3.9 percent, with the greatest number of affected individuals between the ages of eighteen and twenty-nine.

Whether children can develop bipolar disorder is a highly controversial issue, with strong feelings on all sides. Some psychiatrists are convinced that the illness does not affect children, saying that they suffer from other conditions and are being misdiagnosed. Others disagree, arguing that bipolar disorder can affect people of all ages, even young children. Fink and Kraynak write: "The diagnosis of bipolar disorder in children (up to the age of 12) and adolescents (teenagers) has been an area of debate and controversy for more than a decade now. Even professionals in the field fundamentally disagree about some features of diagnosing this disorder in young age groups."[12]

What Causes Bipolar Disorder?

As with other mental illnesses, exactly what causes bipolar disorder is unknown. But years of research have yielded numerous discoveries, from which scientists have derived theories about causes. Genetics, for instance, is believed to play a role in who develops bipolar disorder. Studies have clearly shown that the illness runs in families, which indicates that genetic factors are involved. Closely related to that is biological vulnerability, which refers to being born with vulnerabilities in the brain that could predispose someone to bipolar disorder or other mental illnesses.

Speaking of mental illness in general, Columbia University professor of brain science Eric Kandel explains: "All mental processes are brain processes, and therefore all disorders of mental functioning are biological diseases. The brain is the organ of the mind. Where else could [mental illness] be if not in the brain?"[13]

> **Lack of sleep is risky for people with bipolar disorder because when they are overtired, this can trigger manic episodes.**

Even experts who are convinced of the link between biological factors and bipolar disorder recognize the likelihood that other factors are involved as well. Some that are believed to play a role in bipolar disorder include stress (emotional or physical), abuse of drugs and alcohol, and/or environmental factors such as toxins in the air and water, diet, and viruses, among others. Scientists say that these factors alone cannot cause bipolar disorder but may work together in complex ways with biological and genetic factors. Clinical psychologist Eric A. Youngstrom explains: "Stress and trauma increase risk, as do intense emotional conflicts in families. Most of the risk factors for bipolar disorder also increase the odds of developing other conditions, such as anxiety or attention problems, which probably is why we see such high rates of co-occurrence among these disorders."[14]

Coexisting Disorders

A common way experts refer to the "co-occurrence" of disorders is by using the medical term *comorbidity*. This is highly relevant to any discussion of bipolar disorder, as it is common for people to suffer from two or more mental illnesses at the same time. In a 2011 paper, psychiatrists Doron Sagman and Mauricio Tohen state that the comorbidity of bipolar disorder and other mental illnesses has "become the rule rather than the exception." They cite several studies, one in which 95 percent of people with bipolar disorder met *DSM* diagnostic criteria for up to three other psychiatric disorders. Most common were anxiety disorders such as panic disorder, post-traumatic stress disorder, phobias, and obsessive-compulsive disorder. "Of these," Sagman and Tohen write, "panic disorder appears to have the highest risk of comorbidity."[15]

For a study published in October 2011, researchers from Walter Reed Army Institute of Research analyzed data from a major survey of hospital discharges from 1979 to 2006. The team found that bipolar disorder patients commonly suffered from other psychiatric conditions, as well as physical diseases. Some of the latter included thyroid disease, viral hepatitis, obesity, migraine headaches, skin diseases, and respiratory illnesses. As the published report states: "These results demonstrate the burden of disease among persons with bipolar disorder and highlight the importance of identifying comorbid conditions in this population."[16]

How Does Bipolar Disorder Affect People's Lives?

Bipolar disorder can be extremely difficult for those who must live with it day after day. The drastic, severe mood swings that are the hallmark of the illness can have a profound effect on their quality of life. One specific problem associated with bipolar disorder is sleep disturbances. During periods of mania people with bipolar disorder may be too revved up to sleep or even see no need for sleep at all. "Sleeping feels like a waste of time," says Miklowitz, "especially when so many things can get accomplished in the middle of the night!" Conversely, the individual with bipolar disorder may want desperately to sleep but be unable to. Miklowitz writes: "Sleep eludes you. You may lie awake at night tossing and turning, thinking about the same problems over and over again, and then feel exhausted the next day. Sleep can feel frustratingly out of your reach."[17] Lack of sleep is risky for people with bipolar disorder because when they are overtired, this can trigger manic episodes.

> **It is essential for bipolar disorder to be diagnosed and treated as early as possible because the condition tends to worsen over time.**

Another problem that is closely associated with bipolar disorder is substance abuse. Although scientists are not certain why the two so often go hand in hand, they do have some theories. One of the most prevalent theories is that bipolar disorder sufferers use alcohol and/or drugs in an attempt to cope with the ongoing challenges and emotional pain of living with the illness. This is known as self-medicating, and rather than help the person cope, it actually raises the risk for a host of new problems. Psychiatrist William R. Marchand writes: "Self-medication almost always makes things worse, sometimes much worse by progressing to a substance use disorder."[18]

The Bipolar Disorder Diagnosis

It is essential for bipolar disorder to be diagnosed and treated as early as possible because the condition tends to worsen over time. According to the NIMH, as time goes by someone who has the illness will likely suffer more frequent and more severe episodes than when it first appeared. Accurately diagnosing bipolar disorder can be extremely challenging, however. Unlike physical illnesses, there are no blood tests, scans, or other medical tests that can detect mental illnesses. Still, patients will undergo a physical examination and variety of laboratory tests so the physician can check for any medical conditions that could be causing bipolar symptoms. These may include blood tests, magnetic resonance imaging or computed tomography scans, and/or tests that check thyroid function and hormone levels.

> Mental health professionals stress that psychotherapy is an important part of treatment for bipolar disorder patients.

Once all underlying medical problems have been ruled out, the physician typically consults with a psychiatrist, who can evaluate the patient for possible mental illness. The bipolar disorder diagnosis is made based on the person's medical history and symptoms, along with criteria spelled out in the DSM. An accurate diagnosis is very important because it ensures that the treatment team can create the most appropriate treatment regimen for the patient.

Treatment Options

Although bipolar disorder treatment varies from person to person, the typical regimen includes a combination of medications and therapy. Often called the first-line treatment for bipolar disorder, these medications

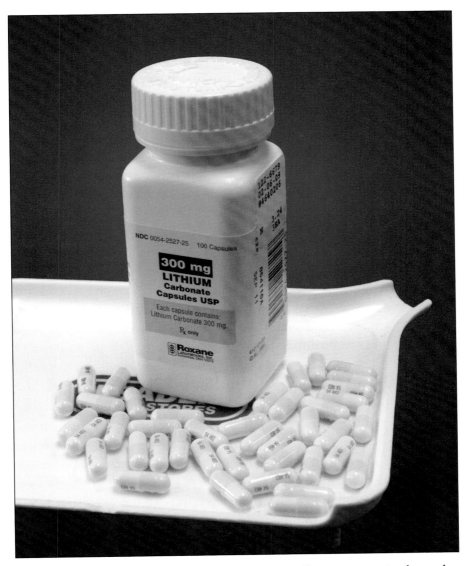

Lithium has been identified as effective in controlling manic episodes and preventing their recurrence in people with bipolar disorder, although scientists are not exactly sure why this is so.

are designed to address biological vulnerabilities, such as correcting flaws in brain chemistry. One example is lithium, a drug that has proved to be effective at controlling manic episodes. Miklowitz says that scientists are not exactly sure why the drug is so effective, but he shares a common theory: "Lithium appears to affect pathways that determine whether chemical messages are sent successfully from the brain to other parts of the body or from one part of the brain to another."[19] Because bipolar disorder is so complex and each patient's needs are unique, most people who have it will try several different medications before finding the most effective ones.

Mental health professionals stress that psychotherapy is an important part of treatment for bipolar disorder patients. There are numerous benefits of therapy, one of which is helping the patient accept his or her illness and learn how best to keep it under control. Also, it can be very difficult for someone to handle the emotional aspects of a severe mental illness, and therapy can help the patient cope with those feelings. According to Marchand, studies have shown that the combination of medication and therapy for people with bipolar disorder is significantly more effective than medication alone. "For example," he says, "there is evidence that adding psychotherapy to medication can decrease the relapse rate by about 40% for bipolar disorder. This is a huge difference in outcome for a disorder that can be difficult to treat."[20]

Can People Overcome Bipolar Disorder?

Bipolar disorder is considered a chronic, lifelong condition, and as frustrating as it can be, sufferers must accept that as their reality. The National Alliance on Mental Illness (NAMI) explains: "As people become familiar with their illness, they recognize their own unique patterns of behavior. If individuals recognize these signs and seek effective and timely care, they can often prevent relapses. But because bipolar disorder has no cure, treatment must be continuous."[21]

The NAMI's reference to continuous treatment means the management of bipolar disorder on a long-term basis, which is called maintenance. Being committed to this is crucial; patients who start feeling good and think they are "cured" may decide to skip their treatment regimen, and this can lead to relapse. Conversely, those who accept their illness and are diligent about sticking with their maintenance program can reap the benefits of those efforts. "Many incredibly talented and productive people have successfully dealt with bipolar disorder," says Youngstrom, "so a goal of treatment should not just be symptom reduction, but helping the person to make the most of their gifts and abilities."[22]

Hurdles and Hope

Bipolar disorder is a complicated, challenging mental illness. Although there are varying degrees of severity, those who have the disorder must cope with moods that swing from the lows of crippling depression to the highs of intense, severe mania. Living with such wild mood fluctuation can seem unbearable at times—but there is hope. With the right treatment program, many people with bipolar disorder can overcome their challenges and lead happy, healthy lives.

What Is Bipolar Disorder?

66 Most people with bipolar disorder describe their moods as volatile, unpredictable, 'all over the map,' or 'like a seesaw.' 99

—David J. Miklowitz, a professor of psychiatry at the University of California–Los Angeles School of Medicine and the author of *The Bipolar Disorder Survival Guide.*

66 With apologies to Charles Dickens, bipolar disorder is often experienced as the 'best of times and the worst of times.' This polarity often causes bipolar disorder to be undiagnosed, overdiagnosed, or misdiagnosed. 99

—Stephen V. Sobel, a psychiatrist from San Diego, California.

I n a June 2012 *Psychology Today* article, British psychiatrist and author Neel Burton presents an interesting depiction of bipolar disorder's long and colorful history. He explains that the depression characteristic of the illness was originally known as "melancholy," a term that traces back to writings of the ancient Greeks. "'Melancholy' derives from *melas* 'black' and *chole* 'bile,'" says Burton, "because Hippocrates thought that depression resulted from an excess of black bile."[23] Burton goes on to say that the word *mania* is also rooted in ancient Greek, with the archaic word *menos* signifying "spirit" and "passion" and *mainesthai* meaning "to rage" or "go mad."

Ancient Wisdom

According to Burton, the ancient Greeks were the first to notice that some individuals suffered from the peculiar combination of melancholy and mania. Specifically he attributes this observation to Aretaeus, a re-nowned Greek physician who lived during the first century CE in Cap-padocia, a region that is now part of Turkey. In his writings Aretaeus spoke of a "miserable form of disease" that afflicted people with two very different symptoms. The first was mania, which Aretaeus referred to as "madness" and "a chronic derangement of the mind."[24]

In describing the effects of mania, Aretaeus spoke of a group of patients who "laugh, play, dance night and day, and sometimes go openly to the market crowned, as if victors in some contest of skill." He went on to de-scribe melancholy, saying that patients who had been suffering from mania sometimes became "dull or stern, de-jected, or unreasonably [lethargic], without any manifest cause: such is the commencement of melancholy."[25]

> " **Mania is an in-tense, heightened emotional state that causes dras-tic mood and be-havioral changes.** "

Aretaeus's descriptions of mania and melancholy were largely accurate, as was his observation that one disease could produce radically different symptoms. Many centuries passed, how-ever, before his theory was accepted by scientists, as Burton writes: "Al-though he suggested that both patterns of behaviour resulted from one and the same disorder, this idea did not gain currency until the modern era."[26]

The "Racing Brain"

Through decades of research, scientists have gained a great deal of knowl-edge about bipolar disorder. But the illness is still mysterious in many ways, which is why continued studies are essential. British scientist Nick Craddock, who refers to bipolar disorder as a "complex, serious and often fatal illness," explains: "Improving the lives of those with bipolar disorder requires an understanding of the causes and triggers of illness. Research is vital."[27] Studies of bipolar disorder have revealed important clues about risk factors and possible causes, problems associated with the illness, and which groups have the highest prevalence. Research has also yielded a vast amount of information about the characteristics of bipolar disorder. For example, scientists now have a good understanding of mania and the many ways that it affects people.

Mania is an intense, heightened emotional state that causes drastic mood and behavioral changes. Some examples include a marked spike in energy levels; a decreased need for sleep; little or no appetite; the inability to focus or pay attention; thoughts that jump erratically from one idea to another; and rapid-fire speech, with frequent interruptions when others are trying to talk. Psychotherapist and author Eric Maisel describes mania as "a racing brain driven by a certain powerful pressure, need or impulse." He goes on to explain a person's thought process while he or she is under the influence of mania: "Anything that gets in the way of this seemingly forward motion—a physical obstacle, another person's viewpoint, a delay in the bus arriving—is viewed as a tremendous irritation. Hence the irritability so often associated with mania. This irritation makes perfect sense: if you *must* get on with it—get every wall painted red, capture that song, solve that theorem—*then nothing must get in the way.*"[28]

> Although most everyone with bipolar disorder suffers from depression, research suggests that those with bipolar II have more frequent depressive episodes than those with bipolar I.

Ashley Prentice Norton vividly remembers a time in her life when she felt controlled by mania. Norton has suffered from bipolar disorder since 1999, when the first symptoms emerged without warning. She and her husband were at a restaurant with friends one evening when suddenly Norton became distracted by some unusual feelings. Because she was not hungry she ordered only toast for dinner, and she found herself enjoying the rough feel of it against her fingers. Then the cracked plastic that covered the menus captured her attention, and she felt an overpowering need to tell everyone about its "poetic beauty."[29] Once Norton started talking, no one else had an opportunity to say anything because she would not give them a chance.

By that point Norton had lost all self-control. She completely dominated the conversation and was unable to stop rambling, as she explains: "Every time someone tries to interrupt me, I slice through their words, talking, talking, and thinking I should be writing all of this down, it is so important. My husband puts his hand on mine and asks if I want to go to the bathroom . . . I say yes, only later understanding he just wanted a break from my incoherent remarks."[30] For Norton, that night proved to be the beginning of a long, painful battle with bipolar disorder.

The Inevitable Crash

One of the most difficult aspects of bipolar disorder is that sufferers must cope with two extremes: the abnormally high points of mania and the low points of depression. Candida Fink and Joe Kraynak write: "A deep depression can wrap you in despair and sentence you to endless days in bed. A full-blown manic episode can buck you like a raging bull and then toss your exhausted carcass. Whether you soar high or plummet down, an extreme, prolonged mood episode can be devastating."[31]

Although most everyone with bipolar disorder suffers from depression, research suggests that those with bipolar II have more frequent depressive episodes than those with bipolar I. British therapist Hannah Leach explains: "It would be over-simplistic to think of this as a milder, less destructive form of bipolar than bipolar I, because the depressed episodes are just as severe and long-lasting. If anything, a bipolar II person may be depressed for much more of the time, which may explain why, statistically, they are more likely to commit suicide than people with any other form of bipolar illness."[32] This is a familiar concept to Nicole Bogdas, a young woman with bipolar II who once came perilously close to taking her own life.

> " **Hospitalizations for children seven to nine years old who were diagnosed with bipolar disorder increased nearly 700 percent from 1997 to 2010.** "

Bogdas first became severely depressed when she was in high school, as she writes: "I was an honors student, captain of the cheerleading squad and editor at the newspaper with a caring boyfriend of almost two years. Life was (supposed to be) good. Yet there I was crying every night."[33] After she was diagnosed with bipolar disorder, it seemed as though life was getting more and more difficult. Finally, by New Year's Eve in 2007, Bogdas had become so despondent that she was preparing to take an overdose of prescription drugs. "I arranged the pill bottles in a neat row and considered my options," she says. That, fortunately, was when Bogdas realized she did not want to die. She says that after staring at the array of drugs she had so meticulously lined up, she "took a deep breath and called a suicide hotline."[34]

Since that night Bogdas has made progress through treatment, and her condition has steadily improved. She freely shares her story with others who may benefit from her experience. "I hope I'm helping," she says. "I want to dispel the myth that all people with mental illness are unproductive or threatening members of society. Maybe someone will see this and find hope, rather than fear, in their lives."[35]

Onset in Adolescence

As was the case with Bogdas, many people with bipolar disorder exhibit their first symptoms as teenagers. According to the NIMH, the illness often develops during a person's late teens or early adult years, with at least half of all cases starting before the age of twenty-five. Examining the prevalence of bipolar disorder among adolescents was the focus of a study that was published in September 2012. Led by NIMH researcher Kathleen Ries Merikangas, the team used data from a nationally representative, face-to-face survey of more than ten thousand teenagers. With diagnostic criteria from the *DSM*, the researchers analyzed the data for symptoms of bipolar disorder (mania and depression) among the teens. The analysis revealed that an estimated 2.5 percent of adolescents met the criteria for bipolar I or II.

> "Since ancient times, when the Greek physician Aretaeus documented his observations about melancholy and mania, bipolar disorder has been studied by scientists throughout the world."

Another finding of the study was that rates of bipolar disorder increased with age. About 2 percent of youth aged thirteen to fourteen reported manic episodes, compared with 3.1 percent of teens aged seventeen to eighteen. According to Merikangas, the study underscores the widely held belief that bipolar disorder first appears during adolescence, as she explains: "I think our data suggest that bipolar disorder is more common in adolescents than previous studies had shown." Although the study does not necessarily prove that bipolar disorder cases among teens are rising, it does indicate that increasing numbers of young people are seeking treatment for psychiatric problems and being diagnosed with bipolar disorder. Says Merikangas: "The take home message is that adolescence is when we really see bipolar disorder begin, so we should shift our focus of prevention and intervention earlier in the lifespan."[36]

The "Bipolar Child"?

It is a common belief among mental health professionals that bipolar disorder first emerges during the adolescent years. What is not so widely accepted is the concept of children developing the illness—yet the number of children who have been diagnosed with bipolar disorder has soared since the mid-1990s. According to a January 2013 report by the Agency for Healthcare Research and Quality, hospitalizations for children seven to nine years old who were diagnosed with bipolar disorder increased nearly 700 percent from 1997 to 2010.

Stuart L. Kaplan, who is a child psychiatrist and clinical professor of psychiatry at Penn State College of Medicine, finds the rising trend of pediatric bipolar disorder diagnoses to be deeply disturbing. "I have been a child psychiatrist for nearly five decades," he says, "and have seen diagnostic fads come and go. But I have never witnessed anything like the tidal wave of unwarranted enthusiasm for the diagnosis of bipolar disorder in children that now engulfs the public and the profession."[37] According to Kaplan, children who are diagnosed with bipolar disorder are being misdiagnosed, which can be dangerous for them. He goes on to say that it is nearly impossible to distinguish between children who are said to have bipolar disorder and those who have "straightforward anger-control issues," as he explains:

> The symptoms may look like mania: irritability, distractibility, and talkativeness. But most of these symptoms can easily be matched to less-trendy conditions like attention-deficit/hyperactivity disorder (ADHD) and oppositional defiant disorder (ODD). My view is that a

diagnosis of bipolar disorder in a child is almost always a case of severe ADHD combined with severe ODD, both fairly common in elementary-school children.[38]

The APA, including the working group that developed the new *DSM*, apparently shares Kaplan's perspective about childhood bipolar disorder. After lengthy deliberations, the group opted to eliminate the diagnosis of pediatric bipolar disorder from the *DSM-5*. Instead, they created a new diagnostic category known as "disruptive mood dysregulation disorder," which is described as intense outbursts and irritability that go beyond normal temper tantrums in young children. A May 2013 fact sheet about the new diagnosis explains: "Too many severely impaired children like this are falling through the cracks because they suffer from a disorder that has not yet been defined. A new diagnosis in the fifth edition of the *Diagnostic and Statistical Manual of Mental Disorders (DSM-5)* aims to give these children a diagnostic home and ensure they get the care they need."[39]

Achievements and Mysteries

Since ancient times, when the Greek physician Aretaeus documented his observations about melancholy and mania, bipolar disorder has been studied by scientists throughout the world. Through this research much has been learned about the illness and its characteristics of mania and depression. Yet with each new discovery, new questions are uncovered as well, meaning that there is much more work to be done.

What Is Bipolar Disorder?

66 At its best, bipolar disorder inspires brilliant insights and uninhibited joy. At its worst, it drapes the mind in debilitating depression. 99

—Candida Fink and Joe Kraynak, *Bipolar Disorder for Dummies*. Hoboken, NJ: Wiley, 2013, p. 11.

Fink is a child and adolescent psychiatrist who specializes in bipolar disorder, and Kraynak is an author whose wife has bipolar disorder.

66 All people with bipolar disorder have manic episodes— abnormally elevated or irritable moods that last at least a week and impair functioning. But not all become depressed. 99

—American Psychological Association, "Bipolar Disorder," 2013. www.apa.org.

The American Psychological Association is a scientific and professional organization that represents the field of psychology in the United States.

* Editor's Note: While the definition of a primary source can be narrowly or broadly defined, for the purposes of Compact Research, a primary source consists of: 1) results of original research presented by an organization or researcher; 2) eyewitness accounts of events, personal experience, or work experience; 3) first-person editorials offering pundits' opinions; 4) government officials presenting political plans and/or policies; 5) representatives of organizations presenting testimony or policy.

❝Manic and hypomanic episodes are generally characterized by excessive elation, known as euphoria.❞

—William R. Marchand, *Depression and Bipolar Disorder: Your Guide to Recovery*. Boulder, CO: Bull, 2012, p. 25.

Marchand is a psychiatrist from Utah and a researcher who focuses on the neurobiology of mood and anxiety disorders.

❝The states of mania and depression can occur in distinct episodes or can switch rapidly, even multiple times in one week.❞

—NAMI, "Bipolar Disorder Fact Sheet," April 2013. www.nami.org.

The NAMI is a grassroots organization that advocates on behalf of those with mental illness and their families.

❝Mood shifts may occur only a few times a year, or as often as several times a day. In some cases, bipolar disorder causes symptoms of depression and mania at the same time.❞

—Mayo Clinic, "Bipolar Disorder," January 18, 2012. www.mayoclinic.com.

The Mayo Clinic is a world-renowned medical facility that is dedicated to patient care, education, and research.

❝People will experience ups and downs in everyday life. What sets bipolar disorder apart is that the swings happen with more frequency and intensity than developmentally appropriate and they last much longer.❞

—Eric A. Youngstrom, interviewed by the American Psychological Association, "Myths and Realities About Bipolar Disorder," American Psychological Association, October 23, 2012. www.apa.org.

Youngstrom is a professor of psychology and psychiatry at the University of North Carolina–Chapel Hill and associate director of the Center for Excellence in Research and Treatment of Bipolar Disorder.

66 The main difference between bipolar disorder and major clinical depression is the presence of manic episodes. This is why depression alone is not enough to diagnose an individual with bipolar. 99

—Brain & Behavior Research Foundation, "Frequently Asked Questions About Bipolar Disorder," 2013. http://bbrfoundation.org.

The Brain & Behavior Research Foundation seeks to fight mental illness by awarding grants that will lead to advances and breakthroughs in scientific research.

....

66 It is well established that bipolar disorder can have childhood onset. Indeed, retrospective studies have found that adult patients report childhood onset in the majority of cases. 99

—Steven R. Pliszka, "Tracking the Development of Bipolar Disorder in Childhood," *American Journal of Psychiatry*, editorial, June 1, 2012. http://ajp.psychiatryonline.org.

Pliszka is a child psychiatrist from San Antonio, Texas.

....

Facts and Illustrations

What Is Bipolar Disorder?

- According to an international study published in the March 2011 issue of *Archives of General Psychiatry*, an estimated **2.4 percent** of adults worldwide suffer from bipolar disorder.

- The NAMI states that bipolar disorder affects more than **10 million** Americans.

- According to the NIMH, at least **half** of all bipolar disorder cases start before the age of twenty-five.

- The Agency for Healthcare Research and Quality reports that hospital stays for childhood bipolar disorder increased **434 percent** from 1997 to 2010.

- The Depression and Bipolar Support Alliance states that an equal number of **men and women** develop bipolar disorder.

- According to clinical psychologist Eric A. Youngstrom, the most prominent way bipolar disorder changes with age is that older people are more likely to experience **depression** and less likely to have **severe mania**, whereas mania is the most prominent characteristic among younger sufferers.

- A 2012 study by researchers from the NIMH found that an estimated **2.5 percent** of adolescents aged thirteen to eighteen met diagnostic criteria for bipolar disorder I or II.

United States Has Highest Incidence of Bipolar Disorder

One of the few studies focused on bipolar disorder on a global scale was published in March 2011 by an international team of researchers. Of the eleven countries surveyed, the United States was found to have the highest incidence of the illness.

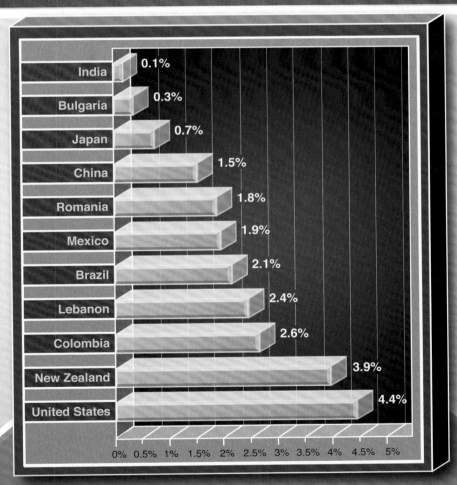

Bipolar Disorder Prevalence in Eleven Countries
(as a percentage of population)

India	0.1%
Bulgaria	0.3%
Japan	0.7%
China	1.5%
Romania	1.8%
Mexico	1.9%
Brazil	2.1%
Lebanon	2.4%
Colombia	2.6%
New Zealand	3.9%
United States	4.4%

Note: In some cases, researchers surveyed particular regions rather than entire countries.

Source: Kathleen R. Merikangas et al. "Prevalence and Correlates of Bipolar Spectrum Disorder in the World Mental Health Survey Initiative," *Archives of General Psychiatry*, March 2011. www.ncbi.nlm.nih.gov.

Bipolar Disorder in US College Population

To better understand the prevalence of various mental illnesses among college students in the United States, the National Alliance on Mental Illness conducted a survey from August to November 2011. Only depression was found to be more prevalent than bipolar disorder among students surveyed.

Diagnosed Mental Illnesses Among College Students

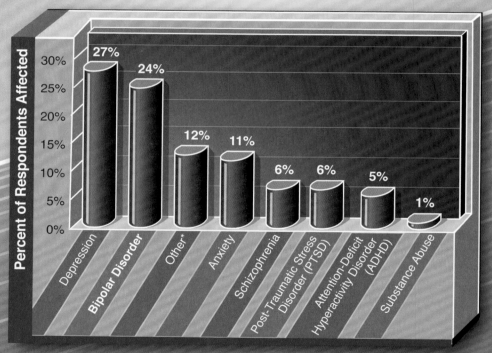

* Other diagnoses include borderline personality disorder, dysthymia, eating disorders, obsessive-compulsive disorder, schizoaffective disorder, and autism spectrum disorder.

Source: National Alliance on Mental Illness, "College Students Speak: A Survey Report on Mental Health," October 30, 2012.

- According to the Anxiety and Depression Association of America, most people with bipolar disorder are symptom free between episodes, but up to one-third still have **lingering symptoms**.

- The United Kingdom's Royal College of Psychiatrists says that bipolar disorder affects about **one person in one hundred** and is less common than depression.

- A study published in the March 2011 issue of *Archives of General Psychiatry* found that worldwide prevalence of bipolar disorder ranged from a low of **0.1 percent** of the population in Nigeria to a high of **4.4 percent** in the United States.

- According to an article by psychiatrist Roxanne Dryden-Edwards, about two-fifths of people with bipolar disorder have at least one bout with **rapid cycling**, which is the occurrence of four or more manic and/or depressive episodes during the previous year.

- Psychologist David J. Miklowitz says the typical age of first onset of bipolar disorder is **eighteen**.

What Causes Bipolar Disorder?

What Causes Bipolar Disorder?

" There are a number of factors that are believed to play a role in developing bipolar disorder including genetics, brain chemicals, environmental factors and sometimes medical illnesses."

—The Black Dog Institute, an Australian organization that offers specialist expertise in the diagnosis, treatment, and prevention of bipolar disorder and other mood disorders.

" All mood disorders start in the brain. Since the brain is an organ of the body, like the heart or the pancreas, mood disorders are physical, biologically-based disorders."

—The Balanced Mind Foundation, which advocates on behalf of families raising children with bipolar disorder and other mood disorders, helping them find answers, support, and stability.

For someone who has just been diagnosed with bipolar disorder, it can be extremely frustrating to hear that no one knows what causes it. Invariably, the patient will want answers that doctors, even those who specialize in mental illness, are unable to provide. David J. Miklowitz writes: "Two major questions plague virtually everyone diagnosed with bipolar disorder: 'How did I get this?' and 'What triggers an episode of mania or depression?' Some people put it more simply: 'What's wrong with my brain?'"[40] Even in the absence of a known cause, scientists have some strong theories about how bipolar disorder develops. Most are convinced that the illness results from multiple factors working together, which Miklowitz refers to as "a complex interplay of genetic background, individual biochemistry, and life stress."[41]

Causes Versus Triggers

As with most mental illnesses, both causes and triggers are involved in the development of bipolar disorder. These terms are often used interchangeably, but they are not necessarily the same. When scientists refer to causes of bipolar disorder, they are talking about biological factors that are responsible for its formation. One example is brain chemistry, which is widely believed to play an integral role in the development of bipolar disorder. Another causative factor is genetics, since bipolar disorder is known to run in families. "But," says Miklowitz, "genetics and biology are not going to be the whole story."[42] What he means is that neither biological nor genetic factors could be solely responsible for causing bipolar disorder, because most people who have these vulnerabilities never develop the illness. That is where triggers come into play.

In people who are biologically and/or genetically predisposed, certain factors are known to trigger manic or depressive episodes. These factors often differ from person to person and may vary widely, as Candida Fink and Joe Kraynak explain: "Triggers can range from situations that feel bad or uncomfortable to those that feel especially exciting or stimulating."[43] Although each person with bipolar disorder is unique, some triggering events have proved to be quite common among sufferers. These include disruptions in sleep, the abuse of alcohol and/or drugs, changes of season, and stressful situations such as work- or school-related conflicts, relationship issues, and financial strain.

> As with most mental illnesses, both causes and triggers are involved in the development of bipolar disorder.

To investigate the most prominent triggering events among a group of young adults with bipolar disorder, researchers from New South Wales, Australia, conducted a study in 2012. In the written report the team explains the importance of its study, saying that being able to identify the precipitants, or triggers, of mania and depression in young adults with bipolar disorder could allow intervention at an earlier stage. This, in turn, could possibly decrease the overall impact that the disorder has on young people's lives. "Therefore," the researchers explain, "the aim of the current study was to identify 'real world' triggers of manic/hypomanic and depressive episodes in young adults."[44]

Nearly two hundred males and females aged eighteen to thirty were involved in the study, and all had been diagnosed with bipolar disorder by a qualified health professional. Participants filled out comprehensive questionnaires, as well as taking part in face-to-face interviews with members of the research team. By the end of the study, the team had accumulated several lists of triggers. The most common triggers associated with the onset of manic or hypomanic episodes included falling in love, the use of stimulant drugs, embarking on a creative project, all-night partying, going on vacation, and listening to loud music. Triggers associated with depressive episodes included stressful life events, general stress, fatigue, sleep deprivation, physical injury or illness, menstruation, and decreases in physical exercise. Some triggers contributed to both manic and depressive episodes, including chaotic situations, change in routine, drinking alcohol, and diet changes.

> A prevailing belief about bipolar disorder is that it is a biological illness, meaning one that develops within the brain and affects brain function.

Clues Within the Brain

A prevailing belief about bipolar disorder is that it is a biological illness, meaning one that develops within the brain and affects brain function. For that reason, researchers studying the illness have considered brain research to be a high priority. They are continuously learning what happens in the brains of individuals who develop bipolar disorder—yet truly understanding the human brain is a daunting challenge for even the most astute scientists. William R. Marchand explains: "The complexity of the brain makes it very difficult for us to comprehend how it functions. In fact, some have called the human brain the most complex structure in the universe. Whether that is true is impossible to know, but it is certainly the most complicated organ in the human body." Marchand adds that because scientists are not entirely certain how a healthy brain works, it has been difficult for them to identify the abnormalities that underlie mood disorders. He writes: "It's like trying to sort out an automobile electrical problem without having a wiring diagram."[45]

Marchand cites two different types of brain abnormalities: those that involve structural problems and those that involve functional problems. The former refers to damage that affects the brain's physical composition, such as head injuries, brain tumors, strokes, or various diseases. Mood disorders, according to Marchand, are widely believed to occur as a result of functional rather than structural problems, as he explains: "By 'functional' I mean that the brain circuitry is not operating correctly. This could occur as a result of problems with the communication between two or more nodes in a circuit. Another possibility is that one specific brain region, or node, is not functioning properly and is disrupting the entire circuit."[46] With his mention of "circuits," Marchand is referring to the brain's "wiring"—the intricate network of connected regions that work together in support of processes such as the ability to see, hear, think, remember, and move.

In some cases the faulty brain wiring associated with bipolar disorder can impair an individual's thoughts and perceptions. This is the case with Robin Mohilner, a psychotherapist from Los Angeles, California, who has lived with bipolar disorder for fifteen years. Even though she is able to control her manic and depressive episodes with medication, keeping her impulsivity in check is a constant challenge. "I have difficulty thinking before I speak," she says. "It does not come naturally to me. As a result, I express my thoughts and emotions impulsively. I practice daily to do my best to think before I speak. Most people don't have to do that." Another challenge for Mohilner is picking up on social cues, and she has learned that many others with bipolar disorder have the same problem. "One of the things we often have in common is the

> " Many years of research have strengthened the scientific theory that genetics play an important role in the development of bipolar disorder. "

feeling like everyone else got a book on all of the social rules and expectations except for us,"[47] she says.

Family Ties

Many years of research have strengthened the scientific theory that genetics play an important role in the development of bipolar disorder. A "bipolar disorder gene" has never been found, but this is not really surprising to scientists. Most are convinced that there is not just one gene; rather, many genes, perhaps even hundreds, may contribute in some way to bipolar disorder's development. Further supporting the genetics link is that bipolar disorder is known to run in families. Miklowitz explains: "If your family tree is dotted with people who have had bipolar disorder or some other mood disorder . . . your vulnerability is high. Likewise, if bipolar disorder or other mood disorders are present in several generations (for example, in your siblings, parents, and grandparents), then your genetic vulnerability is higher than that of a person with bipolar disorder in only one generation."[48]

> "One research focus is investigating the link between exposure to certain illnesses by pregnant women and the incidence of bipolar disorder in their children."

According to a June 2013 WebMD article, some of the most convincing data about bipolar disorder's genetic link have come from research with twins. In studies with identical twins, for instance, scientists have learned that if one has bipolar disorder, the other twin has a much higher likelihood of also developing it than other siblings in the family. The article states: "Researchers conclude that the lifetime chance of an identical twin (of a bipolar twin) to also develop bipolar disorder is about 40% to 70%."[49]

In May 2013 a long-term genetics study was published by a team of researchers from Netherlands. It involved monitoring 108 young people who, at the beginning of the study, ranged in age from twelve to twenty-one and who all had parents with bipolar disorder. The researchers performed psychiatric evaluations on each participant after one year, five years, and twelve years, when the study ended. They found that 54 percent had developed some type of mood disorder, with 13 percent of them meeting diagnostic criteria for bipolar disorder. From this data, the researchers concluded that the risk of developing mood disorders is significantly higher among people whose parents had bipolar disorder than for those whose parents did not.

A Genetic Breakthrough

In February 2013 the largest genetic study of mental illnesses ever conducted was published in the British medical journal *Lancet*. The focus of the study, which involved a team of scientists from eighty research centers in twenty countries, was to investigate whether genetic variations were unique to individual psychiatric disorders or possibly shared across disorders. The study took six years and involved an in-depth analysis of genetic data from more than 61,000 people worldwide: 33,332 with mental illnesses and (for comparison) 27,888 without. The illnesses examined in the study were bipolar disorder, schizophrenia, autism, major depression, and attention-deficit/hyperactivity disorder (ADHD). Scientists performed an analysis to see if people with these illnesses had any distinctive patterns in their DNA.

By the conclusion of the study, the researchers had discovered that the five psychiatric disorders shared several of the same genetic abnormalities. The team could see that these abnormalities accounted for up to 28 percent of the risk for developing one of the illnesses. The particular illness someone develops will vary depending on environmental factors or perhaps other genetic factors. According to Jordan Smoller, senior scientist in the Broad Institute's Stanley Center for Psychiatric Research, this is a major finding that could have widespread implications for further research on the role of genetics in causing mental illnesses. "What we identified here is probably just the tip of an iceberg," he says. "As these studies grow we expect to find additional genes that might overlap."[50]

Risk to the Unborn

In their quest to determine the causes of bipolar disorder, scientists pursue many types of studies, including those that go beyond brain chemistry and genetics. One research focus is investigating the link between exposure to certain illnesses by pregnant women and the incidence of bipolar disorder in their children. This was the purpose of a study that was funded by the NIMH and published in May 2013 by researchers from Columbia University and New York State Psychiatric Institute. At the conclusion of the study, the team had strong evidence that if expectant mothers contract influenza, it can cause severe problems for their unborn children.

The study involved following a group of children who were born in a Northern California county between 1959 and 1966. The researchers identified ninety-two of them who had developed bipolar disorder and compared the rates of maternal flu diagnoses during pregnancy with a group who had not developed the illness. The team discovered that when women contracted flu during pregnancy, it quadrupled the child's risk for developing bipolar disorder later in life. In a news release about the study, researcher Alan Brown said that only a small fraction of pregnant women are immunized for influenza, and that needs to change. He feels strongly that expectant mothers need to take "common sense preventive measures, such as getting flu shots prior to and in the early stages of pregnancy and avoiding contact with people who are symptomatic."[51]

Chipping Away at the Mystery

Bipolar disorder is an illness with many unknowns, and its cause is one of those unknowns. Research points to biological factors such as problems with brain circuitry as well as genetics, since the illness is known to run in families. A number of triggers are also involved, and these act as catalysts for the onset of manic and depressive episodes. With all the research that has been done throughout the years, scientists have gained a much greater understanding of bipolar disorder. Still, they cannot say with total certainty what causes it.

Primary Source Quotes*

What Causes Bipolar Disorder?

66 Bipolar disorder is a mood disorder caused by a chemical imbalance in the brain. 99

—Palo Alto Medical Foundation, "Bipolar Disorder," 2013. www.pamf.org.

The Palo Alto Medical Foundation is a health-care organization that serves the California counties of Alameda, San Mateo, Santa Clara, and Santa Cruz.

66 Although bipolar disorder is a physical illness that affects the brain, referring to its cause as a 'chemical imbalance' is misleading. 99

—Candida Fink and Joe Kraynak, *Bipolar Disorder for Dummies.* Hoboken, NJ: Wiley, 2013, p. 19.

Fink is a child and adolescent psychiatrist who specializes in bipolar disorder, and Kraynak is an author whose wife has bipolar disorder.

* Editor's Note: While the definition of a primary source can be narrowly or broadly defined, for the purposes of Compact Research, a primary source consists of: 1) results of original research presented by an organization or researcher; 2) eyewitness accounts of events, personal experience, or work experience; 3) first-person editorials offering pundits' opinions; 4) government officials presenting political plans and/or policies; 5) representatives of organizations presenting testimony or policy.

> **"Family history has long been recognized as an important clinical feature of bipolar disorder."**
>
> —Huaiyu Yang, "Decoding the Biology of Bipolar Disorder: An Update on Recent Findings in Genetics, Imaging, and Immunology," *Focus*, Fall 2011. http://psychiatryonline.org.

Yang is a psychiatrist with Sierra Pacific Mental Illness Research Education and Clinical Centers in Palo Alto, California.

> **"There are scientists all around the world looking for the genes responsible for bipolar illness and major depression."**
>
> —Kay Redfield Jamison, in Grace Bello, "A Conversation with Kay Redfield Jamison, Professor of Psychiatry," *Atlantic*, November 11, 2011. www.theatlantic.com.

Jamison is a professor of psychiatry at Johns Hopkins School of Medicine and a noted authority on bipolar disorder, which she has battled for a number of years.

> **"Brain imaging and other types of studies are helping uncover differences in the brains of people with bipolar disorder. The significance of these differences is still uncertain."**
>
> —Joe Krucik, "What Do You Want to Know About Bipolar Disorder?," Healthline, September 25, 2013. www.healthline.com.

Krucik is a physician from San Francisco, California.

> **"As with most other mental disorders, bipolar disorder is not directly passed from one generation to another genetically. Rather, it is the result of a complex group of genetic, psychological, and environmental factors."**
>
> —Roxanne Dryden-Edwards, "Bipolar Disorder (Mania)," MedicineNet, June 12, 2012. www.medicinenet.com.

Dryden-Edwards is a psychiatrist from Gaithersburg, Maryland.

❝We know that inheriting bipolar disorder can't be as simple as inheriting brown hair or blue eyes. Too many people with the disorder do not have relatives with mood disorders.❞

—David J. Miklowitz, *The Bipolar Disorder Survival Guide*. New York: Guilford, 2011, p. 79.

Miklowitz is a professor of psychiatry at the University of California–Los Angeles School of Medicine and senior clinical researcher at Oxford University in the United Kingdom.

❝At this point, research has identified lots of genes that each contribute a little bit of risk for bipolar disorder.❞

—Eric A. Youngstrom, interviewed by the American Psychological Association, "Myths and Realities About Bipolar Disorder," American Psychological Association, October 23, 2012. www.apa.org.

Youngstrom is a professor of psychology and psychiatry at the University of North Carolina–Chapel Hill and associate director of the Center for Excellence in Research and Treatment of Bipolar Disorder.

❝People with bipolar disorder appear to have physical changes in their brains. The significance of these changes is still uncertain but may eventually help pinpoint causes.❞

—Mayo Clinic, "Bipolar Disorder," January 18, 2012. www.mayoclinic.com.

The Mayo Clinic is a world-renowned medical facility that is dedicated to patient care, education, and research.

Facts and Illustrations

What Causes Bipolar Disorder?

- According to the NIMH, some imaging studies have shown that there are distinct **differences in the brains** of people with bipolar disorder compared with those of healthy individuals.

- A 2013 study by researchers from Denmark and the United States found that the risk of developing a mood disorder increases by **62 percent** for people who have been hospitalized for an infectious disease.

- According to Palo Alto, California, psychiatrist Huaiyu Yang, it is widely accepted that many genes, each with small effects, cumulatively contribute to the formation of bipolar disorder, but **no single gene** has been identified.

- Child and adolescent psychiatrist Linda Chokroverty says that children with a parent or sibling who has bipolar disorder are **six to ten times** more likely to develop it than children without a family history of the condition.

- According to the Brain & Behavior Research Foundation, too much of the chemical known as **glutamate** in the brain can ultimately impair the health of neurons (brain cells), and this can play a role in the development of bipolar disorder.

- Psychiatrist William R. Marchand states that mood disorders (including bipolar disorder) are generally believed to result from **functional causes**, meaning brain circuitry that is not operating correctly.

A Complex Interaction

Unlike diseases that have a clear-cut cause, bipolar disorder's cause is unknown. The prevailing theory among scientists is that a combination of factors lead to the development of bipolar disorder.

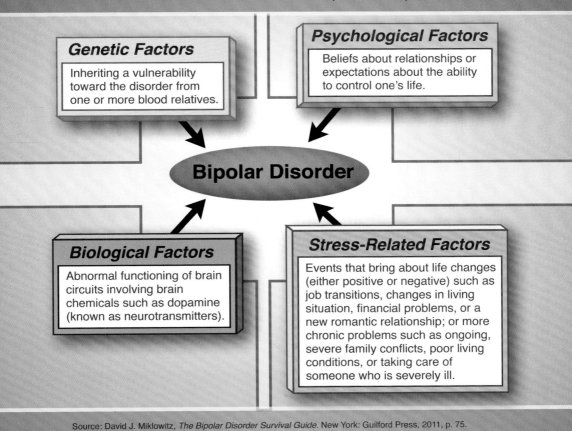

Genetic Factors

Inheriting a vulnerability toward the disorder from one or more blood relatives.

Psychological Factors

Beliefs about relationships or expectations about the ability to control one's life.

Bipolar Disorder

Biological Factors

Abnormal functioning of brain circuits involving brain chemicals such as dopamine (known as neurotransmitters).

Stress-Related Factors

Events that bring about life changes (either positive or negative) such as job transitions, changes in living situation, financial problems, or a new romantic relationship; or more chronic problems such as ongoing, severe family conflicts, poor living conditions, or taking care of someone who is severely ill.

Source: David J. Miklowitz, *The Bipolar Disorder Survival Guide*. New York: Guilford Press, 2011, p. 75.

- A 2013 study led by Broad Institute senior scientist Jordan Smoller found that bipolar disorder and four other psychiatric disorders (autism, ADHD, major depression, and schizophrenia) share some of the same **genetic risk factors**.

A Hereditary Mental Illness

Bipolar disorder is known to run in families, which indicates that genetics play a role in its development. One study that supports this theory was conducted between 2006 and 2009 by researchers who assessed a group of youths between the ages of twelve and twenty-one. As this graph shows, participants with any form of bipolar disorder were those who had at least one parent with the illness.

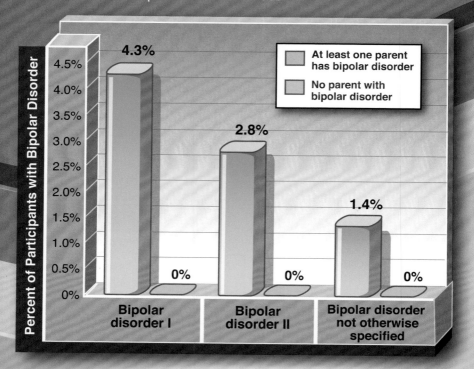

Note: Bipolar I and II are similar disorders, except that people with the latter suffer from hypomania (which is a less severe form of mania).

Source: John I. Nurnberger et al. "A High-Risk Study of Bipolar Disorder," *Archives of General Psychiatry*, October 2011. http://archpsyc.jamanetwork.com.

- According to clinical psychologist Eric A. Youngstrom, research has identified a **number of genes** that could each contribute a little bit of risk for bipolar disorder.

Mood Episode Triggers

Identifying some of the most common triggers of bipolar disorder was the focus of a study published in 2012. That study involved nearly two hundred young adults who have been diagnosed with bipolar disorder. Shown here are the factors the study identified as most often triggers mood episodes. Mood episodes include mania (a state of hyper-excitability), hypomania (a milder form of mania), and depression.

Triggers specific to mania/hypomania	Triggers specific to depression	Triggers common to both
• Falling in love • Recreational stimulant use • Starting a creative project • Period of personal growth • Partying all night • Going on vacation • Listening to loud music • Spring season • Energy drinks • Antidepressant medication • Sugar • Caffeine • Allergy medication	• Stressful life events • General stress • Fatigue • Sleep deprivation • Physical injury/illness • Menstruation • Decreased exercise	• Routine change • Chaotic situations • Alcohol • Diet change • Marijuana • Jetlag • Cigarettes • Flu medication

Source: Judith Proudfoot, Alexis Whitton, Gordeon Parker, Justin Doran, Vijaya Manicavasagar, Kristy Delmas, "Triggers of Mania and Depression in Young Adults with Bipolar Disorder," *Journal of Affective Disorders*, December 2012, pp. 196–202.

- A June 2013 WebMD paper states that the brain chemicals **serotonin and noradrenaline** have consistently been linked to psychiatric disorders such as depression and bipolar disorder.

- According to the United Kingdom's Royal College of Psychiatrists, **stress** can trigger manic or depressive episodes in people with bipolar disorder.

How Does Bipolar Disorder Affect People's Lives?

66 **Individuals with bipolar disorder can quickly swing from extremes of happiness, energy and clarity to sadness, fatigue and confusion. These shifts can be so devastating that individuals may choose suicide.** 99

—American Psychological Association, a scientific and professional organization that represents the field of psychology in the United States.

66 **People living with or caring for someone with bipolar disorder can have a tough time. During episodes of illness, the personalities of people with bipolar disorder may change, and they may become abusive or even violent.** 99

—National Health Service, the health-care system of the United Kingdom.

Julianna Shapiro knows from personal experience how difficult it can be to live with bipolar disorder. She has battled the illness for more than twenty years, and for the most part is able to keep it under control with medications. Still, she is not symptom free. Even now she sometimes has what she calls "breakthrough manias," or manic episodes that come on despite the medications she takes to help prevent them. "None of us is perfect or impervious to the evils of this disorder," she says. "And to be clear, two words are important here: evil and disorder."

When Shapiro does have a manic episode, it leads to a loss of control that she sums up in one word: "miserable." And at the risk of angering those who would take issue with her, she says that the sheer misery of this "often times crippling disease"[52] is the one thing people with bipolar disorder share in common.

Anything but "Fun"

Shapiro can usually sense when she is about to have a manic episode, although she is never sure exactly when it will hit her "full tilt." When it does, she feels a sudden burst of energy and becomes physically and mentally agitated. She finds that her speech is "pushed" and she cannot slow it down or stop talking. From there it gets worse, as she explains: "After several hours of the mania, it builds to a point where my skin starts to itch from the inside. I just want out of myself. I want to paralyze my tongue from all of the talking. I can't sit still, I am squirming, and sometimes this makes me anxious. At this point, all I want is for it to stop."[53] If Shapiro does not get the mania under control by taking medicine, she becomes argumentative, combative, and even mean to people.

> **According to Shapiro, anyone who has the impression that mania is 'fun' is badly misinformed.**

With mania being such a dreadful experience for her, Shapiro finds it exasperating when she hears some people glorifying it as though it were something to cheer about. She has even heard mania described as "fun," and she says nothing could be further from the truth. "If your idea of fun is having your brain put in a food processor on high for hours or days, sure," she says. "If you don't value eating or sleeping, yep, big fun. If your goal is to lose friends and alienate people, big time carnival right there. If you want a giant depressive crash (not right away) sometime afterward, then YES, mania is a blasty blast." According to Shapiro, anyone who has the impression that mania is "fun" is badly misinformed. "No one wants this, and no one needs this," she says. "If it were a good thing it would not be an illness and we would not need medication to set the path straight again."[54]

An Unfair Reality

Christiane Wells, a social worker from Highlands Ranch, Colorado, who has bipolar disorder, agrees that the word *fun* has no place in any description of the illness. "One fallacy is that mania is always a great time, and I assure you it is not," she says. "Sometimes a manic episode manifests as extreme agitation, and the feeling is so uncomfortable it makes me want to jump out of my skin."[55]

One of Wells's biggest frustrations is how misunderstood bipolar disorder is and how stigmatized people are who have it. This is true even though celebrity sufferers such as Carrie Fisher, Howie Mandel, Demi Lovato, Russell Brand, and Catherine Zeta-Jones have spoken out about their own struggles with the disorder. Their openness has helped increase awareness and acceptance of mental illness, but the stigma issue is still a significant problem. Wells writes: "The misconceptions surrounding bipolar disorder are many, and until they are dispelled, stigma will continue to cause people to suffer alone—hesitant or fearful to admit that they have a mental illness lest their friends, family and coworkers discover they are 'crazy.'"[56]

> " Stigmatization is known to be a serious problem for many who suffer from mental illness. "

At her last place of employment, Wells worked as a caseworker for child protection, and she chose not to tell anyone that she had bipolar disorder. She was dismayed to notice that her coworkers often made degrading remarks about clients who had the illness, and this deeply hurt her. "They had no idea (yet) about my own struggle with bipolar disorder," says Wells, "and didn't realize they might as well have been talking about me." Eventually, she became so depressed that she needed to take time off "before I completely fell apart"—and she ended up losing her job. "Once my boss and the administrators knew, it was over," she says. "I was labeled 'crazy,' and that was that."[57]

Unfortunately, Wells's experience is not that uncommon, even today when there are antidiscrimination laws in place to protect people. Stigmatization is known to be a serious problem for many who suffer from mental illness. To better understand the magnitude of the problem, a team of researchers from Queen's University in Ontario, Canada, conducted a study in 2011. Participants included 214 individuals aged twenty to seventy who had been diagnosed with either bipolar disorder or depression. They all completed questionnaires and were also personally interviewed by members of the research team.

After results were compiled, the team found that a high percentage of participants had experienced many types of stigma-related problems, and this had negatively affected their quality of life. Although coping with stigmatization was a problem for people in both groups, it appeared to have a greater impact on those with bipolar disorder. Of that group, the two worst problems identified were the perceptions that people are afraid of them because of their mental illness and that people think less of those who have a mental illness. Many with bipolar disorder said they tried to avoid situations that could be stigmatizing for them and felt that their experiences with stigma affected how they felt about themselves and/or their abilities.

> " People with bipolar disorder who become violent may have reached the point of psychosis, which means they have lost their grip on reality. "

In the written report, which was published in 2012, the researchers explain how the study helped them better understand the stigma problem from the "perspective of people who are affected by mental illness." The conclusion they drew from their research illustrates the extent of the problem: "The experience of stigma associated with mental illness is devastating and can be detrimental to recovery."[58]

The Danger Factor

In keeping with society's penchant for stigmatizing people with bipolar disorder, the belief that those who suffer from it are unpredictable and dangerous is not uncommon. Even though the fears are often exaggerated and based on myths rather than facts, there is a kernel of truth to that perception. Writer Madeline Vann, who holds a masters degree in public health, refers to this issue as "complicated," saying that between 11 and 16 percent of people with bipolar disorder have had some type of violent episode. "These typically occur during extreme moods or because of drug or alcohol use," she says. "But there are many people with bipolar disorder who are never violent. Knowing which bipolar symptoms of depression and mania to watch out for may help avoid dangerous situations."[59]

People with bipolar disorder who become violent may have reached the point of psychosis, meaning they have lost their grip on reality. A common effect of psychosis is delusions, which are irrational, unshakable beliefs in something that is untrue. Closely related are hallucinations, during which sufferers see, hear, smell, or feel things that they believe are real but do not actually exist. Most often these are auditory hallucinations, whereby the person hears voices that no one else can hear, and this can be terribly disturbing. Clinical psychologist Tali Shenfield writes: "Acute symptoms of psychosis can be dangerous and damaging to others, as well as the person suffering from them, because the individual loses control over thoughts, feelings and behaviors."[60]

To evaluate the frequency of violent behavior among people with bipolar disorder or schizophrenia, New York University School of Medicine psychiatry professor Jan Volavka conducted a study in 2012. Titled "Violence in Schizophrenia and Bipolar Disorder," the study was sorely needed, according to Volavka, as he writes: "In spite of its obvious practical importance, violence in psychiatric patients has attracted relatively little attention in the literature."[61]

The study involved a comprehensive search using the National Institute of Health's MEDLINE database for articles published between 1966 and November 2012. After compiling the data and performing an in-depth examination, Volavka concluded that the risk of violence in patients with either mental illness was greater than in the general population. He also learned that the problem was worse among people with bipolar disorder, as he explains: "The evidence suggests that the risk of violence is greater in bipolar disorder than in schizophrenia."[62] Volavka goes on to say that most often, violent acts committed by people with bipolar disorder occurred during periods of extreme mania.

Impaired Health and Premature Death

The link between bipolar disorder and emotional problems has been well established and is rarely questioned. But a major study published in July 2013 revealed something that was not so widely known: Sufferers are more likely to develop serious illnesses and die at younger ages than those without bipolar disorder.

The study was conducted by Casey Crump, who is a clinical assistant professor of medicine at Stanford School of Medicine, and his colleagues. The team analyzed data on more than 6.5 million people living in Sweden between 2003 and 2009, including 6,618 who suffered from bipolar disorder. The team found that, on average, people with bipolar disorder died about nine years younger than those in the general population. The various diseases that increased their risk of dying included heart disease, respiratory diseases, diabetes, influenza, and pneumonia. For women with bipolar disorder, cancer was also a higher risk than for the general population. Crump's team cannot say for certain why these diseases affected people with bipolar disorder at such high rates, but theories include failure to seek medical attention, unhealthy diet, smoking, and substance abuse, among other possible factors.

> **It has long been known that suicide rates among people with mental illness, including bipolar disorder, are alarmingly high.**

High Risk of Suicide

In addition to serious illness, Crump's team also found that a major cause of premature death among bipolar disorder sufferers was suicide. This finding was not unexpected, since it has long been known that suicide rates among people with mental illness, including bipolar disorder, are alarmingly high. Says Kluger: "Rates of suicide are significantly higher among people with bipolar disorder than their peers."[63] In the study by Crump and his colleagues, women with bipolar disorder were found to be ten times more likely to kill themselves than people in the general population, and men were nine times more likely.

According to Suzanne Hudson, who is chief executive of the United Kingdom–based group Bipolar UK, bipolar disorder has the highest rate of suicide of any mental illness. In 2012 her organization, along with the Royal College of Psychiatrists and Bipolar Scotland, conducted a survey of 706 people with bipolar disorder. The group found that only 15 percent of the participants had been diagnosed promptly, whereas the remaining 85 percent waited an average of thirteen years before being correctly diagnosed. Of those whose diagnosis was delayed, 71 percent said that their symptoms had become worse over time. The researchers say this was likely due to their being misdiagnosed with depression and receiving inappropriate treatment such as antidepressants, which can worsen manic episodes. "A delay of this length has a significant impact for individuals and families," says Hudson, "with sometimes devastating consequences."[64]

No Easy Life

Although no two people with bipolar disorder face exactly the same challenges, there is ample evidence that it is tough to live with. Sufferers must endure stigmatization and are often forced to hide their illness because of it. They have a higher-than-normal risk of contracting many diseases, tend to die at younger ages, and have a high risk of suicide. For those who are suffering from bipolar disorder, Shapiro offers these words of advice: "Let's take our meds and do our very best to be stable. . . . See the doctor, take our medications, manage our lives."[65]

Primary Source Quotes*

How Does Bipolar Disorder Affect People's Lives?

Bipolar disorder is associated with a significantly elevated risk of suicide. Moreover, bipolar patients often use highly lethal means for suicide.

—Stephen V. Sobel, "Effective Personalized Strategies for Treating Bipolar Disorder," *Psychiatric Times*, August 2, 2012. www.psychiatrictimes.com.

Sobel is a psychiatrist from San Diego, California.

Delusions and hallucinations are particularly scary to significant others, who view them as the most concrete sign of 'craziness.'

—David J. Miklowitz, *The Bipolar Disorder Survival Guide*. New York: Guilford, 2011, p. 24.

Miklowitz is a professor of psychiatry at the University of California–Los Angeles School of Medicine and senior clinical researcher at Oxford University in the United Kingdom.

* Editor's Note: While the definition of a primary source can be narrowly or broadly defined, for the purposes of Compact Research, a primary source consists of: 1) results of original research presented by an organization or researcher; 2) eyewitness accounts of events, personal experience, or work experience; 3) first-person editorials offering pundits' opinions; 4) government officials presenting political plans and/or policies; 5) representatives of organizations presenting testimony or policy.

"Mood disorders are very serious and disabling conditions."

—William R. Marchand, *Depression and Bipolar Disorder: Your Guide to Recovery*. Boulder, CO: Bull, 2012, p. 2.

Marchand is a psychiatrist from Utah and a researcher who focuses on the neurobiology of mood and anxiety disorders.

"One of the more challenging issues for young adults with bipolar disorder involves the prospect of finding a fulfilling and enduring love relationship."

—Russ Federman, "Finding Love with Bipolar Disorder: Those Nasty Perceptions of Damaged Goods," *Psychology Today*, May 15, 2011. www.psychologytoday.com.

Federman is a psychologist from Charlottesville, Virginia, who specializes in patients with bipolar disorder.

"Suicide is far more common among teenagers and young adults than most of us are aware. Tragically, most of these young people have a completely treatable, biologically-based illness like clinical depression or bipolar disorder."

—Balanced Mind Foundation, "Frequently Asked Questions," 2013. www.thebalancedmind.org.

The Balanced Mind Foundation advocates on behalf of families raising children with bipolar disorder and other mood disorders, helping them find answers, support, and stability.

"The worst thing for me about manic-depression is that it is simply free-floating. You can have no reason whatsoever, and yet you are in the depths of an inarticulatable sadness and grief and self-hatred."

—Richard Dreyfuss, "Richard Dreyfuss Talks About Living with Bipolar Disorder," *Sarasota (FL) Herald-Tribune*, April 3, 2011. http://health.heraldtribune.com.

Dreyfuss is an actor who has starred in movies, television shows, and live theater, and who suffers from bipolar disorder.

66 **Whether you soar high or plummet down, [an] extreme, prolonged mood episode can be devastating to your relationships, career, and other aspects of your life.** 99

—Candida Fink and Joe Kraynak, *Bipolar Disorder for Dummies.* Hoboken, NJ: Wiley, 2013, p. 13.

Fink is a child and adolescent psychiatrist who specializes in bipolar disorder, and Kraynak is an author whose wife has bipolar disorder.

66 **Mood swings with bipolar I cause significant difficulty in your job, school or relationships. Manic episodes can be severe and dangerous.** 99

—Mayo Clinic, "Bipolar Disorder," January 18, 2012. www.mayoclinic.com.

The Mayo Clinic is a world-renowned medical facility that is dedicated to patient care, education, and research.

How Does Bipolar Disorder Affect People's Lives?

- According to the World Health Organization, bipolar disorder is the sixth leading cause of **disability** worldwide.

- The NAMI says that untreated bipolar disorder sufferers not only experience more frequent or more severe episodes, but also suffer **higher death rates** from medical conditions such as cancer, heart disease, and stroke.

- A major international study published in the March 2011 issue of *Archives of General Psychiatry*, found that **50 to 75 percent** of people with bipolar disorder reported severe impairment in daily functioning.

- The NIMH states that people with bipolar disorder have a higher-than-normal likelihood of having **migraine headaches**, which may trigger mania or depressive episodes.

- According to Ohio psychiatrist Adele C. Viguera, **hypersexuality** (sex addiction) is a common symptom when people with bipolar disorder experience manic episodes.

- In a 2011 paper psychiatrists Doron Sagman and Mauricio Tohen state that the risk of **violent behavior** is elevated among people with coexisting bipolar disorder and substance abuse.

Bipolar I Carries Highest Suicide Risk

In general, people who suffer from mental illness have a much higher risk of suicide than those in the general population. A 2012 study conducted by researchers from Spain and the United States found that people with bipolar disorder I have a markedly higher incidence of suicidal thoughts and attempts than those who suffer from bipolar II or depression.

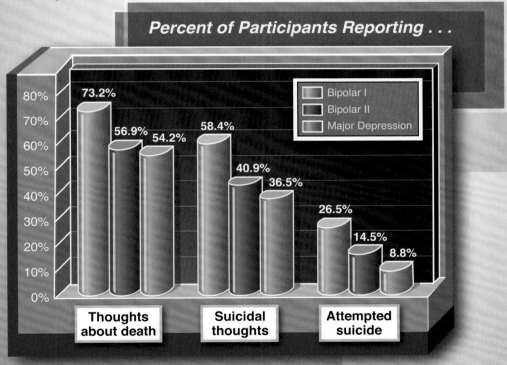

Percent of Participants Reporting . . .

Source: Carmen Moreno, et al. "Depression in Bipolar Disorder Versus Major Depressive Disorder: Results From the National Epidemiologic Survey on Alcohol and Related Conditions," *Bipolar Disorder*, May 2012. www.ncbi.nlm.nih.gov.

- According to the American Academy of Child & Adolescent Psychiatry, one in four people with bipolar disorder will attempt **suicide** at least once, and one in ten will ultimately die by suicide.

The Pain of Being Stigmatized

Coping with the stigma associated with mental illness can be very painful. To evaluate the extent to which people with bipolar disorder and depression feel stigmatized, researchers from Queen's University in Ontario, Canada, conducted a study and published it in 2012. This graph shows some of the difficulties people with bipolar disorder regularly encounter.

Stigma-Related Problems Experienced by People with Bipolar Disorder

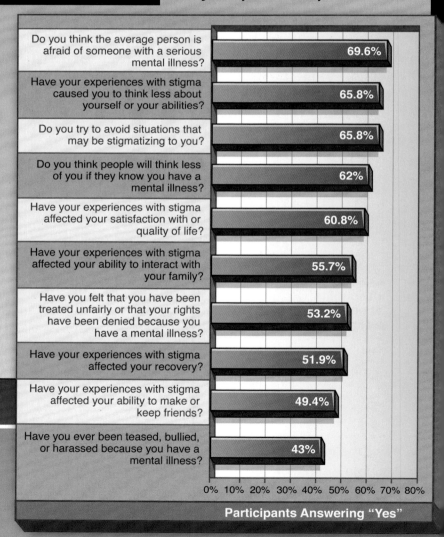

Question	Participants Answering "Yes"
Do you think the average person is afraid of someone with a serious mental illness?	69.6%
Have your experiences with stigma caused you to think less about yourself or your abilities?	65.8%
Do you try to avoid situations that may be stigmatizing to you?	65.8%
Do you think people will think less of you if they know you have a mental illness?	62%
Have your experiences with stigma affected your satisfaction with or quality of life?	60.8%
Have your experiences with stigma affected your ability to interact with your family?	55.7%
Have you felt that you have been treated unfairly or that your rights have been denied because you have a mental illness?	53.2%
Have your experiences with stigma affected your recovery?	51.9%
Have your experiences with stigma affected your ability to make or keep friends?	49.4%
Have you ever been teased, bullied, or harassed because you have a mental illness?	43%

0% 10% 20% 30% 40% 50% 60% 70% 80%

Participants Answering "Yes"

Source: L. Lazowski et al. "Stigma and Discrimination in People Suffering with a Mood Disorder: A Cross-Sectional Study," *Depression Research and Treatment*, 2012. www.hindawi.com.

- According to psychiatrist Roxanne Dryden-Edwards, the number of individuals with bipolar disorder who commit suicide is **sixty** times higher than that of the general population.

- The Mayo Clinic states that people with bipolar disorder are more likely than healthy individuals to develop **physical health problems** such as heart disease and obesity.

- The American Academy of Child & Adolescent Psychiatry states that up to **60 percent** of people with bipolar disorder abuse alcohol or drugs at some point in the course of their illness.

- According to the Anxiety and Depression Association of America, **anxiety** is a common complication of bipolar disorder and a significant trigger of manic episodes.

- The NIMH states that people with bipolar disorder often have **thyroid gland problems**, and treatment with the mood-stabilizing drug lithium may cause abnormally low thyroid levels.

Can People Overcome Bipolar Disorder?

"Even the most insightful, self-aware, self-accepting bipolar individual will still experience some mixture of highs, lows and/or irritability that will be difficult to manage. That's life with bipolar disorder."

—Russ Federman, a psychologist from Charlottesville, Virginia, who specializes in patients with bipolar disorder.

"Is there a cure? Short answer, no. Long answer, bipolar disorder is not something that needs to be 'cured.' It's a disorder that needs to be controlled."

—Sylvia Meier, a woman who suffers from bipolar disorder and is the author of several books about her experiences with the illness.

Logan Noone was diagnosed with bipolar disorder in 2011 after spending five days in a psychiatric hospital. To his surprise, he was strongly urged by doctors as well as his fellow patients to keep quiet about his illness. Everyone warned Noone to be careful about whom he told because people would invariably discriminate against him, and in the process, his career could be ruined. "It was really frustrating for me," he says, "because I thought, 'Yeah, but they might not.'" As reluctant as he was, however, Noone took people's advice and told no one about his diagnosis—and after six months of silence, he could not stand to go on like that anymore. He felt himself spiraling into the worst depression he had ever experienced, and his sense of shame became unbearable. "I didn't think I could be anything successful," he says. "I didn't have the drive to get better because I thought I was destined for suicide."[66]

A Life Turned Around

Finally, in early 2013 Noone decided he was fed up and would no longer remain silent about his illness. "I thought, 'I'm not going to live this life anymore,'" he says. "'This is stupid, and I'm not going to be ashamed.'" Two days after moving to California for a job transfer, he told his new roommates about his bipolar disorder and then steeled himself for their rebuttal—only to find that they thought nothing about it. They were completely accepting of him and were glad he had opened up to them. "They taught me the lesson that I'm just a normal guy," he says, "and I can still fit in with everyone else. We all have something wrong with us; no one's DNA is perfect."[67]

Being able to be open and honest about his bipolar disorder and be accepted by his roommates made a remarkable difference in how Noone felt. Suddenly, it was as though he had a renewed purpose in life that he could see clearly. He knew that he was going to help others with bipolar disorder realize that they are not alone and should never be ashamed of their illness. He began attending group meetings for people with bipolar disorder and other mental health issues, listening to the experiences of others and sharing his own experiences and insight. "This was the key to my recovery," he says, "I didn't feel all alone."[68]

> " Medications are also an important part of bipolar disorder treatment because they help control the symptoms; specifically, they help keep the episodes of depression and mania or hypomania under control. "

Today Noone is involved with the advocacy organization Mental Health America and travels to colleges to give speeches about his experience with overcoming bipolar disorder. He recorded a video of one of his speeches and uploaded it to YouTube, in the hopes of spreading his message online to increase awareness and educate people about bipolar disorder. "We're going to try to tell the success stories," he says. "The stories people need to hear. The truth."[69]

Seeking the Ideal Regimen

Like others with bipolar disorder, before Noone started down the path of recovery, he had to find the right treatment program that fit his individual needs. As is typical for people who have the illness, what worked for Noone was a combination of psychotherapy and medications. This is a common treatment regimen, because the two methods are designed to complement each other. Regarding the psychotherapy component, psychiatrist Stephen V. Sobel writes: "Psychotherapy is an integral part of the effective treatment of bipolar disorder."[70] He goes on to say that therapy focuses on a number of different areas, including bipolar disorder education, adherence to medication, and interpersonal relationships.

Medications are also an important part of bipolar disorder treatment because they help control the symptoms; specifically, they help keep the episodes of depression and mania or hypomania under control. Sobel calls mood-stabilizing drugs "the backbone of treatment,"[71] and he says they are loosely organized into three categories: lithium, which has proved to be a very effective drug for controlling mania and preventing the recurrence of mood episodes; antipsychotics, which also help prevent severe mania as well as controlling psychosis; and anticonvulsants, which are often prescribed for treatment during the maintenance phase.

Antidepressants such as Paxil and Prozac may also be prescribed to treat bipolar disorder, but the practice is controversial. Bipolar patients should take these drugs only if they also take mood stabilizers. If antidepressants alone are taken, they can spark a full-blown manic episode. Another risk is that the patient will develop what is known as rapid cycling, a dangerous situation in which he or she alternates between manic and depressive episodes a number of times in a year.

Owen's Story

Before Owen Whalen was diagnosed with bipolar disorder, he experienced a bout of rapid cycling that was immensely frightening for him. Although he was only eleven years old, Whalen had been haunted by such a deep sense of despair that he tried to take his own life. Because of his young age, doctors did not consider that he might be bipolar and misdiagnosed him with major depression. He was given two antidepressants at the hospital and sent home with a third. His mother, Alison, explains: "He came home on a Tuesday, and by Saturday he'd had 11 cycles. We were frantic."[72]

Alison had done a tremendous amount of research and was convinced that her son had bipolar disorder. He had most of the diagnostic criteria that had been established for the illness. His mood swings were severe and frequent. And he was having psychotic symptoms, including frightening hallucinations about an evil man who was shadowing him at school. Finally, a psychiatrist named Barbara Gracious diagnosed Owen with bipolar disorder, and this was a relief to both him and his mother. Although it took a lot of experimenting before the right combination of medications was found, when it finally was, Owen began to make excellent progress. Within two years of his diagnosis his condition had stabilized, and in the fall of 2011 he started college at Rochester Institute of Technology in Rochester, New York.

> " Whether someone with bipolar disorder can recover through holistic treatment methods alone is highly controversial. "

Natural Techniques

Whether someone with bipolar disorder can recover through holistic treatment methods alone is highly controversial. Some alternative medicine specialists are convinced that this is indeed possible. One example is the ketogenic diet, which is a low-carbohydrate and low-protein eating plan that has been touted for regulating unstable moods. Emily Deans, a psychiatrist from Massachusetts, was a bit guarded about this treatment method because it had not been proved through a randomized controlled trial. Then she reviewed two well-documented cases in which women diagnosed with bipolar II were successfully treated with the ketogenic diet, and she was impressed. She writes:

> All in all, the paper is a nice illustration of two motivated patients achieving remission of their bipolar symptoms (which they had dealt with for decades) with a free-living

ketogenic diet (and some other supplements, though each woman took different ones, for example, probiotics and omega 3). Two anecdotes isn't a huge amount of data, but it is intriguing, and I would say the time for a randomized controlled trial of ketogenic diets in bipolar disorder is way overdue.[73]

Unlike Deans, many scientists and physicians are unwilling even to consider the notion that bipolar disorder could be treated successfully with dietary changes. They feel so strongly about the importance of medications to treat bipolar disorder that they scoff at the very idea of alternative methods. Writer Michael Ellsberg found this out for himself while searching for an effective treatment for his bipolar disorder. During a meeting with a psychiatrist, he asked whether the psychiatrist thought there was any link between nutrition and mental health. Ellsberg writes: "He looked at me like I had just asked whether there was any link between mental health and UFO rectal probes. 'There is absolutely *no* evidence of *any link whatsoever* between dietary choices and mental health,' he said curtly, and changed the subject."[74]

> **Many scientists and physicians are unwilling even to consider the notion that bipolar disorder could be treated successfully with dietary changes.**

Ellsberg, however, had learned through experimenting with his diet that the foods he ate made a drastic difference in how he felt. Of particular note were refined sugar (regular white table sugar) and refined or processed carbohydrates such as packaged cereals, white bread, pasta, candy and other sweets, and white rice. After medications had no effect on his bipolar symptoms, Ellsberg became so distraught that he was ready to commit suicide. He was unwilling to give up, however, and eventually found a doctor named Ronald Hoffman, who runs the Hoffman Center in New York City. Hoffman and his staff combine traditional medicine with complementary techniques such as acupuncture, nutrition and vitamin therapy, allergy testing and treatment, and other methods.

Ellsberg did not alter his lifestyle to adopt the holistic method right away. He actually rejected it at first, thinking that giving up some of his favorite foods and beverages would be too difficult. But when his depression continued to deepen and he seriously contemplated jumping out of a fourth-story window, he knew he had to do something drastic. His personal challenge was one year with no refined sugar, no coffee, and no alcohol. He says the "first two weeks of the quest were hell," but he stuck with it, and slowly it began to get easier. In the third week he woke up in the morning feeling very different. "The haze in my mind had lifted," he says. "It was a clear, crisp, brilliant sunny day in my mind—the first such day of sunny internal weather for years." When a year was over, Ellsberg had no intention of giving up his newfound diet plan. "What came out of my year without sugar, coffee, or alcohol?" he asks. "I got my life back."[75]

> A combination of medications has long been considered the mainstay of bipolar disorder treatment, but exactly how these drugs produce their effects has been somewhat of a mystery.

Close to a Cure?

A combination of medications has long been considered the mainstay of bipolar disorder treatment, but exactly how these drugs produce their effects has been somewhat of a mystery. A study announced in April 2013 by researchers from the University of Michigan has helped reveal what might be going on. The team examined brain tissue of fourteen deceased people who had bipolar disorder and twelve who had no mental health conditions. Seven of the brains were from bipolar disorder patients who had been taking one or more antipsychotic drugs at the time of their death. Most had also been taking other types of medications, such as antidepressants.

Through genetic analysis, the researchers compared the gene activity patterns among the brains of bipolar disorder patients who had been exposed to antipsychotics with patterns among those who were not—and they saw remarkable differences. The next step was to compare activity patterns of patients who had been taking antipsychotics with those of people without bipolar disorder, which resulted in similar patterns. Says Melvin McInnis, a University of Michigan psychiatrist who helped lead the study: "We found there are hundreds of genes whose activity is adjusted in individuals taking medication—consistent with the fact that there are a number of genes that are potentially amiss in people with bipolar. Taking the medications, specifically . . . antipsychotics, seemed to normalize the gene expression pattern in these individuals so that it approached that of a person without bipolar."[76] Although it is too soon to say for sure, the study suggests that this could possibly lead to a treatment that corrects the brain problems characteristic of bipolar disorder.

"Recovery Is a Process"

Bipolar disorder is a challenging, often difficult illness for those who suffer from it. There are many treatment options available, ranging from traditional medications and psychotherapy to alternative and complementary methods. And even though the illness can seem unbearable sometimes, the prognosis is certainly not all gloom and doom. The main thing people with bipolar disorder need to accept is that they have a permanent, lifelong condition that requires vigilance and commitment. Says the NAMI: "One of the most important principles of recovery is this: recovery is a process, not an event. The uniqueness and individual nature of recovery must be honored. While serious mental illness impacts individuals in many challenging ways, the concept that all individuals can move toward wellness is paramount."[77]

Primary Source Quotes*

Can People Overcome Bipolar Disorder?

> **Many people with bipolar disorder can now live productive lives and achieve levels of happiness and fulfillment they never dreamed possible.**

—Candida Fink and Joe Kraynak, *Bipolar Disorder for Dummies*. Hoboken, NJ: Wiley, 2013, p. 11.

Fink is a child and adolescent psychiatrist who specializes in bipolar disorder, and Kraynak is an author whose wife has bipolar disorder.

> **It is my strong belief that people who do best with [bipolar] disorder are those who have learned to recognize triggers for their mood cycles and how to minimize the impact of these triggers.**

—David J. Miklowitz, *The Bipolar Disorder Survival Guide*. New York: Guilford, 2011, p. viii.

Miklowitz is a professor of psychiatry at the University of California–Los Angeles School of Medicine and senior clinical researcher at Oxford University in the United Kingdom.

* Editor's Note: While the definition of a primary source can be narrowly or broadly defined, for the purposes of Compact Research, a primary source consists of: 1) results of original research presented by an organization or researcher; 2) eyewitness accounts of events, personal experience, or work experience; 3) first-person editorials offering pundits' opinions; 4) government officials presenting political plans and/or policies; 5) representatives of organizations presenting testimony or policy.

66 **Bipolar disorder causes havoc in patients' lives. Even in the best of circumstances, successful treatment is challenging.** 99

—Stephen V. Sobel, "Effective Personalized Strategies for Treating Bipolar Disorder," *Psychiatric Times*, August 2, 2012. www.psychiatrictimes.com.

Sobel is a psychiatrist from San Diego, California.

66 **Sometimes it takes a little time, but almost everyone with a mood disorder can get better and stay well for life.** 99

—William R. Marchand, *Depression and Bipolar Disorder: Your Guide to Recovery*. Boulder, CO: Bull, 2012, p. 14.

Marchand is a psychiatrist from Utah and a researcher who focuses on the neurobiology of mood and anxiety disorders.

66 **While no cure exists for bipolar disorder, it is treatable and manageable with psychotherapy and medications.** 99

—Brain & Behavior Research Foundation, "Frequently Asked Questions About Bipolar Disorder," 2013. http://bbrfoundation.org.

The Brain & Behavior Research Foundation seeks to fight mental illness by awarding grants that will lead to advances and breakthroughs in scientific research.

66 **The recovery journey is unique for each individual.** 99

—NAMI, "Bipolar Disorder Fact Sheet," April 2013. www.nami.org.

The NAMI is a grassroots organization that advocates on behalf of those with mental illness and their families.

66 In most cases, bipolar disorder can be controlled with medications and psychological counseling. 99

—Mayo Clinic, "Bipolar Disorder," January 18, 2012. www.mayoclinic.com.

The Mayo Clinic is a world-renowned medical facility that is dedicated to patient care, education, and research.

66 Therapy has a lot of promise as a way of preventing progression of bipolar disorder, delaying relapse, and improving functioning in between episodes. 99

—Eric A. Youngstrom, interviewed by the American Psychological Association, "Myths and Realities About Bipolar Disorder," American Psychological Association, October 23, 2012. www.apa.org.

Youngstrom is a professor of psychology and psychiatry at the University of North Carolina–Chapel Hill and associate director of the Center for Excellence in Research and Treatment of Bipolar Disorder.

Facts and Illustrations

Can People Overcome Bipolar Disorder?

- Funded by the NIMH, a major 2011 study called STEP-BD found that slightly **more than half** of the people treated for bipolar disorder recovered (meaning having fewer than two symptoms for at least eight weeks) within a one-year period.

- A study published in March 2011 by an international team of researchers found that fewer than half of those with bipolar disorder received mental health treatment; in the lowest-income countries, only **25 percent** reported contact with the mental health system.

- According to the NAMI, the most useful **psychotherapies** for people with bipolar disorder are those that focus on understanding the illness, learning how to cope with it, and changing ineffective patterns of thinking or interacting.

- In an August 2012 paper, psychiatrist Stephen V. Sobel explains that the depression in bipolar disorder has proved to be **more resistant to medication** treatment than mania.

- Clinical psychologist Eric A. Youngstrom says that the most effective bipolar disorder treatments focus on **smoothing out the highs and lows** in mood and energy.

- According to the Black Dog Institute, a world leader in the diagnosis, treatment and prevention of mood disorders such as depression and bipolar disorder, many people with bipolar disorder are **not accurately diagnosed** for ten years or more.

Treatment Worldwide Is Tied to Income

A study conducted by a team of international researchers examined bipolar disorder prevalence in eleven countries. Of the topics covered, one was the availability of treatment. The study found that people in low- to middle-income countries are much less likely to receive treatment for bipolar disorder than people in high-income countries.

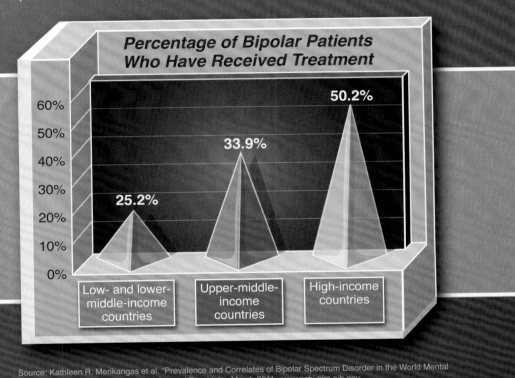

Percentage of Bipolar Patients Who Have Received Treatment

Source: Kathleen R. Merikangas et al. "Prevalence and Correlates of Bipolar Spectrum Disorder in the World Mental Health Survey Initiative," *Archives of General Psychiatry*, March 2011. www.ncbi.nlm.nih.gov.

- The NAMI states that even though bipolar disorder often has natural periods of remission, those who meet criteria for the disorder will almost always **relapse** without treatment.

- According to psychiatrist Roxanne Dryden-Edwards, **aerobic exercise** has been found to help alleviate some of the thinking problems that are associated with bipolar disorder, such as **poor memory** and an **inability to pay attention**.

The Value of Psychotherapy

Although medications are often referred to as the mainstay of bipolar disorder treatment, mental health specialists stress that most patients would also benefit greatly from one or more types of therapy. This table shows some psychotherapy types that have proved to be effective in treating people with bipolar disorder.

Type of Psychotherapy	Description/Purpose
Cognitive behavioral therapy	Teaches the patient to pay attention to automatic positive thoughts as potential triggers for hypomania or mania
Dialectical behavior therapy	Helps patient work toward improving the regulation of emotions
Psychoeducational therapy	Helps patient understand triggers and techniques for managing his or her illness
Family-focused therapy	Helps the patient and family members improve communication and reduce intense emotional conflict
Interpersonal social rhythm therapy	Emphasizes regular sleep and activity patterns

Source: Eric A. Youngstrom, interviewed by the American Psychological Association, "Myths and Realities About Bipolar Disorder," American Psychological Association, October 23, 2012. www.apa.org.

- The Anxiety and Depression Association of America states that when a patient suffers from both bipolar disorder and an anxiety disorder, most doctors first prescribe a **mood stabilizer** to address the bipolar disorder.

- According to the NIMH, in recent years **electroconvulsive therapy** (formerly called shock treatment) has been shown to provide relief for people with severe, treatment-resistant bipolar disorder.

Psychotherapy Rated Highest by Bipolar Disorder Patients

In a survey conducted by the health information sharing group known as CureTogether, 227 people with bipolar disorder shared their experiences with a variety of different treatments. As this graph shows, participants rated psychotherapy the highest, followed by exercise.

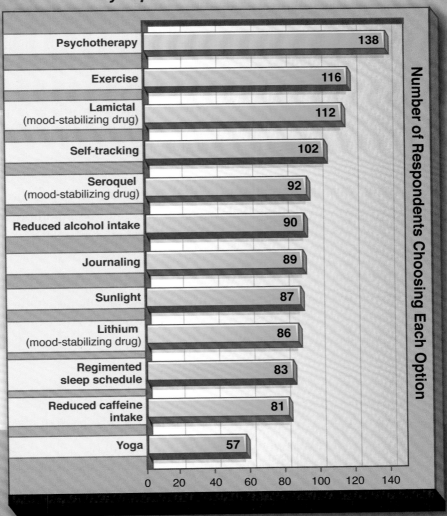

Top Twelve Treatments Chosen by Bipolar Disorder Patients

Treatment	Number of Respondents Choosing Each Option
Psychotherapy	138
Exercise	116
Lamictal (mood-stabilizing drug)	112
Self-tracking	102
Seroquel (mood-stabilizing drug)	92
Reduced alcohol intake	90
Journaling	89
Sunlight	87
Lithium (mood-stabilizing drug)	86
Regimented sleep schedule	83
Reduced caffeine intake	81
Yoga	57

Source: Alexandria Carmichael, "Bipolar Managed Best Without Drugs: 227 Patients Report," CureTogether, February 15, 2012. http://curetogether.com.

Key People and Advocacy Groups

American Psychiatric Association: The main professional organization of psychiatrists and trainee psychiatrists in the United States and the largest psychiatric organization in the world.

Joseph Biederman: A Harvard Medical School psychiatrist who published accounts of bipolar disorder in young children that led to a substantial increase in pediatric bipolar disorder diagnoses, along with an accompanying rise in the use of antipsychotic drugs to treat the condition. In 2011 Biederman was reprimanded for failing to disclose his paid consultancy arrangement with pharmaceutical companies that make the drugs, which was a conflict of interest.

John F.J. Cade: An Australian psychiatrist and researcher who in 1949 became the first to treat patients with a chemical known as lithium, which eventually became the primary treatment for mania.

Depression and Bipolar Support Alliance: An advocacy organization that seeks to provide hope, help, support, and education to improve the lives of people with bipolar disorder and other mood disorders.

Sigmund Freud: A renowned Austrian neurologist who believed that factors such as childhood trauma and unresolved developmental conflicts were at the root of mental illness; he became known as the father of psychoanalysis and was the first to use it in treating patients with the illness that later became known as bipolar disorder.

Kay Redfield Jamison: A professor of psychiatry at Johns Hopkins School of Medicine and a noted authority on bipolar disorder who was instrumental in increasing awareness of the illness with her 1995 memoir, *An Unquiet Mind,* a book about her own battle with bipolar disorder.

Karl Ludwig Kahlbaum: A German psychiatrist who was among the first to recognize manic-depressive illnesses as a unique disorder and who coined the term *cyclothymia*.

Stuart L. Kaplan: A child psychiatrist and clinical professor of psychiatry at Penn State College of Medicine who is well known for his outspoken belief that bipolar disorder does not affect young children.

Emil Kraepelin: A German psychiatrist who first introduced the term *manic-depressive insanity* to describe mania, as well as the first to differentiate between schizophrenia and manic depression; Kraepelin observed that the former was chronic and deteriorating, whereas manic depression was episodic with a return to normal functioning between episodes.

Karl Leonhard: A German psychiatrist who in 1957 coined the terms *bipolar* for patients with depression and mania and *unipolar* for patients who suffer from depressive episodes only.

National Alliance on Mental Illness: An organization that is dedicated to improving the lives of people who suffer from mental illness, as well as the lives of their families.

National Institute of Mental Health: An agency of the National Institutes of Health and the largest scientific organization in the world dedicated to research on mental disorders and the promotion of mental health.

Eric A. Youngstrom: A professor of psychology and psychiatry at the University of North Carolina–Chapel Hill and associate director of the Center for Excellence in Research and Treatment of Bipolar Disorder.

Chronology

1913
In his book *General Paresis*, Emil Kraepelin establishes that manic-depressive illness includes recurrent, severe depression combined with periods of mania.

1621
English scholar Robert Burton releases *The Anatomy of Melancholy*, a book that describes melancholy (now known as depression) as a mental illness.

1946
US president Harry S. Truman signs the National Mental Health Act, which calls for the establishment of a mental health agency that will conduct research in order to help reduce mental illness. Three years later this leads to the formation of the National Institute of Mental Health.

1817
Swedish chemist Johan August Arfvedson discovers the chemical element lithium in an iron mine in Stockholm, Sweden.

1600   **1800**   **1900**   **1935**   **1970**

1686
Swiss physician Théophile Bonet coins the term *manico-melancolicus* for what would eventually become known as manic depression.

1896
In the first edition of his psychiatry textbook, German psychiatrist Emil Kraepelin introduces the term *manic-depressive insanity* to describe the grandiose delusions associated with mania.

1957
German psychiatrist Karl Leonhard coins the terms *bipolar* for patients with depression and mania and *unipolar* for patients who suffer from depressive episodes only.

1949
Australian psychiatrist and researcher John F.J. Cade reports on the dramatic improvement of ten manic-depressive patients after experimental treatment with lithium.

1853
In a published paper, French psychiatrist and neurologist Jules Gabriel François Baillarger describes "dual-form insanity," which comes to be known as manic depression.

1952
The American Psychiatric Association publishes the first *Diagnostic and Statistical Manual of Mental Disorders* (*DSM*), which includes a category called "manic-depressive reactions."

1970
The US Food and Drug Administration approves lithium for the treatment of manic depression.

1995
In her book titled *The Suicide of My Son*, author Trudy Carlson publishes the first account of a child's painful struggle with bipolar disorder.

2010
A study by National Institute of Mental Health researchers finds that an intravenous dose of the anesthetic drug known as ketamine provided relief to people with treatment-resistant bipolar disorder in as little as forty minutes.

1980
"Bipolar disorder" replaces "manic-depressive disorder" as a diagnostic term in the third version of the *Diagnostic and Statistical Manual of Mental Disorders* (*DSM-III*).

2009
A study by University of Missouri researchers finds that nearly half of those diagnosed with bipolar disorder between the ages of eighteen and twenty-five may outgrow the disorder by the time they reach thirty.

1970   1980   1990   2010

1994
The fourth edition of the *Diagnostic and Statistical Manual of Mental Disorders* (*DSM-IV*) includes a subtype of bipolar disorder known as bipolar disorder II.

2005
A study by researchers from the University of Pittsburgh School of Medicine finds that during the first few years after diagnosis, bipolar disorder is a more severe illness for children than for adults.

2000
The National Depressive and Manic-Depressive Association survey of individuals with bipolar disorder finds that 69 percent of participants were misdiagnosed and more than one-third waited ten or more years before receiving an accurate diagnosis.

2012
Researchers from Emory University School of Medicine in Atlanta, Georgia, announce a study in which patients with treatment-resistant bipolar disorder benefited from a targeted therapy known as deep brain stimulation.

2013
A major study by a consortium of researchers from nineteen countries finds that there are common genetic links across five major psychiatric illnesses: bipolar disorder, ADHD, autism, major depressive disorder, and schizophrenia.

Related Organizations

American Academy of Child & Adolescent Psychiatry (AACAP)

3615 Wisconsin Ave. NW
Washington, DC 20016-3007
phone: (202) 966-7300 • fax: (202) 966-2891
website: www.aacap.org

Composed of more than eight thousand psychiatrists and other interested physicians, the AACAP's members actively research, evaluate, diagnose, and treat psychiatric disorders. Its website's "Bipolar Disorder Resource Center" offers an extensive collection of information about the illness through articles, fact sheets, video clips, and links to other resources.

American Psychological Association

750 First St. NE
Washington, DC 20002-4242
phone: (202) 336-5500; toll-free: (800) 374-2721
website: www.apa.org

The American Psychological Association is a scientific and professional organization that represents the field of psychology in the United States. Its website links to newspaper articles, research data, and a number of online publications that focus on bipolar disorder.

Balanced Mind Foundation

730 N. Franklin St., Suite 501
Chicago, IL 60654-7225
phone: (847) 492-8510
e-mail: info@thebalancedmind.org
website: www.thebalancedmind.org

The Balanced Mind Foundation advocates on behalf of families raising children with bipolar disorder and other mood disorders, helping them find answers, support, and stability. Its website offers news articles, fact sheets, "Library" and "Education Corner" sections, a "Flipswitch" section designed for teens, and links to online support groups.

Brain & Behavior Research Foundation

90 Park Ave., 16th Floor
New York, NY
phone: (646) 681-4888; toll-free: (800) 829-8289
e-mail: info@bbrfoundation.org • website: http://bbrfoundation.org

The Brain & Behavior Research Foundation seeks to fight mental illness by awarding grants that will lead to advances and breakthroughs in scientific research. Its website features news articles; a "Discoveries" section that covers research, technology, diagnostic tools, and therapies; and real-life stories about people who have recovered from bipolar disorder.

Depression and Bipolar Support Alliance

730 N. Franklin St., Suite 501
Chicago, IL 60654-7225
phone: (800) 826-3632 • fax: (312) 642-7243
e-mail: info@dbsalliance.org • website: www.dbsalliance.org

The Depression and Bipolar Support Alliance seeks to provide hope, help, support, and education to improve the lives of people with bipolar disorder and other mood disorders. Its website offers general information about bipolar disorder as well as brochures, podcasts, and videos.

International Bipolar Foundation (IBF)

8895 Towne Centre Dr., Suite 105-360
San Diego, CA 92122
phone: (858) 764-2496 • fax: (858) 764-2491
website: www.internationalbipolarfoundation.org

The International Bipolar Foundation seeks to eliminate bipolar disorder through the advancement of research and to provide and enhance care for those affected by the illness. Its website offers news articles, fact sheets, educational videos, the *My Support* e-newsletter, and a search engine that produces additional materials.

Juvenile Bipolar Research Foundation

7 Whitney St. Extension
Westport, CT 06880
phone: (203) 226-2216 • fax: (203) 341-0496
e-mail: dpapolos@jbrf.org • website: http://bipolarchild.com

The Juvenile Bipolar Research Foundation is the first charitable foundation dedicated to the support of research for the study of early onset bipolar disorder. Its website offers articles about bipolar disorder in children and adolescents, as well as a link to the organization's blog where more information can be found.

Mayo Clinic

200 First St. SW
Rochester, MN 55905
phone: (507) 284-2511 • fax: (507) 284-0161
website: www.mayoclinic.com

The Mayo Clinic is a world-renowned medical facility that is dedicated to patient care, education, and research. The search engine of its website produces a wide variety of publications about bipolar disorder.

Mental Health America

2000 N. Beauregard St., 6th Floor
Alexandria, VA 22311
phone: (703) 684-7722; toll-free: (800) 969-6642 • fax: (703) 684-5968
website: www.mentalhealthamerica.net

Mental Health America is dedicated to helping people live mentally healthier lives and educating the public about mental health and mental illness. The website offers numerous publications about bipolar disorder and other mood disorders.

National Alliance on Mental Illness (NAMI)

3803 N. Fairfax Dr., Suite 100
Arlington, VA 22203
phone: (703) 524-7600; toll-free: (800) 950-6264 • fax: (703) 524-9094
website: www.nami.org

The NAMI is dedicated to improving the lives of people who suffer from mental illness, as well as the lives of their families. Its website features fact sheets, news releases, online discussion groups, and a search engine that produces an assortment of publications on bipolar disorder.

National Institute of Mental Health (NIMH)

Science Writing, Press, and Dissemination Branch
6001 Executive Blvd., Room 8184, MSC 9663
Bethesda, MD 20892-9663
phone: (301) 443-4513; toll-free: (866) 615-6464 • fax: (301) 443-4279
e-mail: nimhinfo@nih.gov • website: www.nimh.nih.gov

An agency of the National Institutes of Health, the NIMH is the largest scientific organization in the world dedicated to research on mental disorders and the promotion of mental health. The "Bipolar Disorder" section of its website covers symptoms, causes, treatments, and clinical trials, and the site's search engine produces a variety of additional materials.

For Further Research

Books

Janelle M. Caponigro et al. , Erica H. Lee, Sheri L. Johnson, and Ann M. Kring, *Bipolar Disorder: A Guide for the Newly Diagnosed*. Oakland, CA: New Harbinger, 2012.

Sylvia Collins, *Long Shot: My Bipolar Life and the Horses Who Saved Me*. New York: HarperCollins, 2011.

Julie A. Fast and John D. Preston, *Loving Someone with Bipolar Disorder*. Oakland, CA: New Harbinger, 2012.

Russ Federman and J. Anderson Thomson Jr., *Facing Bipolar: The Young Adult's Guide to Dealing with Bipolar Disorder*. Oakland, CA: New Harbinger, 2010.

Candida Fink and Joe Kraynak, *Bipolar Disorder for Dummies*. Hoboken, NJ: Wiley, 2013.

Linea Johnson and Cinda Johnson, *Perfect Chaos: A Daughter's Journey to Survive Bipolar, a Mother's Struggle to Save Her*. New York: St. Martin's Griffin, 2013.

David J. Miklowitz, *The Bipolar Disorder Survival Guide: What You and Your Family Need to Know*. New York: Guilford, 2011.

Melody Moezzi, *Haldol and Hyacinths: A Bipolar Life*. New York: Penguin Group, 2013.

Periodicals

Elaine Aradillas, "A *Saved by the Bell* Star's Sad Spiral," *People*, October 15, 2012.

Barbara Brotman, "Bipolar II Disorder—Another Chicagoan's Story," *Chicago Tribune*, August 26, 2012.

Victoria A. Brownworth, "Done with Crazy: How One Lesbian Fought Mental Illness and Lived to Tell the Tale," *Curve*, October 2012.

Sharon Cotliar and Michelle Tauber, "Her Private Struggle," *People*, May 2, 2011.

Dan Hyman, "Passion Pit Singer on Battling Mental Illness and Taking New Songs on the Road," *Rolling Stone*, August 4, 2012.

Stuart L. Kaplan, "Mommy, Am I Really Bipolar?," *Daily Beast*, June 27, 2011.

Elizabeth Leonard, "Carrie Fisher's Bipolar Crisis: 'I Was Trying to Survive,'" *People*, March 25, 2013.

Linda Logan, "The Problem with How We Treat Bipolar Disorder," *New York Times Magazine*, April 26, 2013.

Jacqueline Marshall, "Children with Bipolar Disorder: Maybe True, Definitely Troubling," *Washington Times*, April 23, 2012.

Ashley Prentice Norton, "Mom Interrupted," *Redbook*, August 2012.

Greg Perez Sr. with Max Adler, "My Struggle Against Bipolar Disorder," *Golf Digest*, September 2011.

Sue Sanders, "A Change of Mind: Living with Bipolar Disorder," *Real Simple*, August 2013.

Andrew M. Seaman, "Bipolar Disorder Tied to Mother's Flu in Pregnancy," *Chicago Tribune*, May 10, 2013.

Melissa Wishart, "Darkness on the Edge of Town: The Hidden Epidemic of Bipolar Disorder," *Investigate HERS* (Auckland, New Zealand), June/July 2013.

Internet Sources

American Psychological Association, "Bipolar Disorder," 2013. www.apa.org/topics/bipolar.

Brain & Behavior Research Foundation, "I Thought Maybe This Was Normal," *Recovery Stories*, September 16, 2011. http://bbrfoundation.org/stories-of-recovery/i-thought-maybe-this-was-normal.

Roxanne Dryden-Edwards, "Bipolar Disorder (Mania)," MedicineNet, June 12, 2012. www.medicinenet.com/bipolar_disorder/article.htm.

Mayo Clinic, "Bipolar Disorder," January 18, 2012. www.mayoclinic.com/health/bipolar-disorder/DS00356.

National Institute of Mental Health, "Bipolar Disorder." www.nimh.nih.gov/health/topics/bipolar-disorder/index.shtml.

Eric A. Youngstrom, interviewed by American Psychological Association, "Myths and Realities About Bipolar Disorder," October 23, 2012. www.apa.org/news/press/releases/2012/10/bipolar-disorder.aspx.

Source Notes

Overview

1. Quoted in Elizabeth Leonard, "Carrie Fisher's Bipolar Crisis: 'I Was Trying to Survive,'" *People*, March 25, 2013, p. 76.
2. Quoted in Leonard, "Carrie Fisher's Bipolar Crisis," p. 78.
3. Quoted in Leonard, "Carrie Fisher's Bipolar Crisis," p. 78.
4. David J. Miklowitz, *The Bipolar Disorder Survival Guide*. New York: Guilford, 2011, p. 15.
5. American Academy of Child & Adolescent Psychiatry, "Bipolar Disorder Resource Center: About," June 2013. www.aacap.org.
6. Miklowitz, *The Bipolar Disorder Survival Guide*, p. 33.
7. Therese J. Borchard, "Bipolar I vs. Bipolar II," *World of Psychology* (blog), Psych Central, April 14, 2011. http://psychcentral.com.
8. Russ Federman, "Is Bipolar II Easier to Live with than Bipolar I?," *Psychology Today*, October 28, 2012. www.psychologytoday.com.
9. Candida Fink and Joe Kraynak, *Bipolar Disorder for Dummies*. Hoboken, NJ: Wiley, 2013, p. 340.
10. Lizzie, "There's Nothing Mild About Cyclothymia," *Mind* (blog), March 26, 2013. www.mind.org.uk.
11. Lizzie, "There's Nothing Mild About Cyclothymia."
12. Fink and Kraynak, *Bipolar Disorder for Dummies*, p. 23.
13. Quoted in Kirsten Weir, "The Roots of Mental Illness," *Monitor on Psychology*, June 2012. www.apa.org.
14. Eric A. Youngstrom, interviewed by American Psychological Association, "Myths and Realities About Bipolar Disorder," October 23, 2012. www.apa.org.
15. Doron Sagman and Mauricio Tohen, "Comorbidity in Bipolar Disorder: The Complexity of Diagnosis and Treatment," Psych Central Professional, 2011. http://pro.psychcentral.com.
16. Natalya S. Weber, Jared A. Fisher, David N. Cowan, and David W. Niebuhr, "Psychiatric and General Medical Conditions Comorbid with Bipolar Disorder in the National Hospital Discharge Survey," *Psychiatric Services*, October 2011. http://psychiatryonline.org.
17. Miklowitz, *The Bipolar Disorder Survival Guide*, p. 26.
18. William R. Marchand, *Depression and Bipolar Disorder: Your Guide to Recovery*. Boulder, CO: Bull, 2012, p. 88.
19. Miklowitz, *The Bipolar Disorder Survival Guide*, p. 107.
20. Marchand, *Depression and Bipolar Disorder*, pp. 199–200.
21. National Alliance on Mental Illness, "Bipolar Disorder," April 2013. www.nami.org.
22. Youngstrom, "Myths and Realities About Bipolar Disorder."

What Is Bipolar Disorder?

23. Neel Burton, "A Short History of Bipolar Disorder," *Hide and Seek* (blog), *Psychology Today*, June 21, 2012. www.psychologytoday.com.
24. Francis Adams, trans., *The Extant Works of Aretaeus, The Cappadocian*. London: Sydenham Society, 1856. www.cappadociabipolar.com.

25. Adams, *The Extant Works of Aretaeus, The Cappadocian.*

26. Burton, "A Short History of Bipolar Disorder."

27. Quoted in Cardiff University, "Understanding Bipolar Disorder," News Centre, February 17, 2010. www.cardiff.ac.uk.

28. Eric Maisel, "Intelligence, Creativity and Mania," *Rethinking Psychology* (blog), *Psychology Today*, June 17, 2012. www.psychologytoday.com.

29. Ashley Prentice Norton, "Mom, Interrupted," *Redbook*, 2012, p. 89.

30. Norton, "Mom, Interrupted," p. 89.

31. Fink and Kraynak, *Bipolar Disorder for Dummies*, p. 12.

32. Hannah Leach, "Do You Understand the Bipolar Spectrum?," *World of Psychology* (blog), *Psych Central*, August 21, 2013. http://psychcentral.com.

33. Nicole Bogdas, "My Painful Struggles with Bipolar Disorder," *USA Today*, February 26, 2012. http://usatoday30.usatoday.com.

34. Bogdas, "My Painful Struggles with Bipolar Disorder."

35. Bogdas, "My Painful Struggles with Bipolar Disorder."

36. Quoted in Reuters, "Bipolar Symptoms May Begin in Teen Years: Study," May 8, 2012. www.reuters.com.

37. Stuart L. Kaplan, "Mommy, Am I Really Bipolar?," *Daily Beast*, June 19, 2011. www.thedailybeast.com.

38. Kaplan, "Mommy, Am I Really Bipolar?"

39. American Psychiatric Association, "Disruptive Mood Dysregulation Disorder," *Diagnostic and Statistical Manual of Mental Disorders*, May 2013. www.dsm5.org.

What Causes Bipolar Disorder?

40. Miklowitz, *The Bipolar Disorder Survival Guide*, p. 74.

41. Miklowitz, *The Bipolar Disorder Survival Guide*, p. 7.

42. Miklowitz, *The Bipolar Disorder Survival Guide*, p. 74.

43. Fink and Kraynak, *Bipolar Disorder for Dummies*, p. 170.

44. Judith Proudfoot, Alexis Whitton, Gordon Parker, Justin Doran, Vijaya Manicavasagar, and Kristy Delmas, "Triggers of Mania and Depression in Young Adults with Bipolar Disorder," *Journal of Affective Disorders*, December 2012, p. 197.

45. Marchand, *Depression and Bipolar Disorder*, pp. 89–90.

46. Marchand, *Depression and Bipolar Disorder*, p. 93.

47. Robin Mohilner, "My Experience of Living with Bipolar Disorder," *Thrive with Bipolar Disorder* (blog), 2011. http://thrivewithbipolardisorder.wordpress.com.

48. Miklowitz, *The Bipolar Disorder Survival Guide*, p. 83.

49. WebMD, "Causes of Bipolar Disorder," June 26, 2013. www.webmd.com.

50. Quoted in Gina Kolata, "5 Disorders Share Genetic Risk Factors, Study Finds," *New York Times*, February 28, 2013. www.nytimes.com.

51. Quoted in ScienceDaily, "Flu in Pregnancy May Quadruple Child's Risk for Bipolar Disorder," May 14, 2013. www.sciencedaily.com.

How Does Bipolar Disorder Affect People's Lives?

52. Julianna Shapiro, "Glorifying Bipolar Mania," *Chronically Awesome* (blog), March 30, 2013. http://chronicallyawesome.org.

53. Shapiro, "Glorifying Bipolar Mania."

54. Shapiro, "Glorifying Bipolar Mania."

55. Christiane Wells, "Living with the Stigma of Mental Illness," *Red Room* (blog), *Huffington Post*, April 23, 2011. www.huffingtonpost.com.
56. Wells, "Living with the Stigma of Mental Illness."
57. Wells, "Living with the Stigma of Mental Illness."
58. L. Lazowski et al. "Stigma and Discrimination in People Suffering with a Mood Disorder: A Cross-Sectional Study," *Depression Research and Treatment*, 2012. www.hindawi.com.
59. Madeline Vann, July 13, 2010. "Are People with Bipolar Disorder Dangerous?," Everyday Health, July 13, 2010. www.everydayhealth.com.
60. Tali Shenfield, "Understanding Psychotic and Bipolar Disorders," *KevinMD* (blog), May 19, 2013. www.kevinmd.com.
61. Jan Volavka, "Violence in Schizophrenia and Bipolar Disorder," *Psychiatria Danubina*, December 23, 2013. www.hdbp.org.
62. Volavka, "Violence in Schizophrenia and Bipolar Disorder."
63. Vann, "Are People with Bipolar Disorder Dangerous?"
64. Quoted in Denis Campbell, "People with Bipolar Disorder May Wait 13 Years for Diagnosis," *Guardian* (London), June 26, 2012. www.theguardian.com.
65. Shapiro, "Glorifying Bipolar Mania."

Can People Overcome Bipolar Disorder?

66. Quoted in Loren Grush, "No Longer Silent: Man with Bipolar Disorder Speaks Up About His Illness, Inspiring Others," Fox News, March 7, 2013. www.foxnews.com.
67. Quoted in Grush, "No Longer Silent."
68. Quoted in Grush, "No Longer Silent."
69. Quoted in Grush, "No Longer Silent."
70. Stephen V. Sobel, "Effective Personalized Strategies for Treating Bipolar Disorder," *Psychiatric Times*, August 2, 2012. www.psychiatrictimes.com.
71. Sobel, "Effective Personalized Strategies for Treating Bipolar Disorder."
72. Quoted in Brain & Behavior Research Foundation, "I Thought Maybe This Was Normal," September 16, 2011. http://bbrfoundation.org.
73. Emily Deans, "Ketogenic Diets and Bipolar Disorder: New Case Studies," *Evolutionary Psychiatry* (blog), October 8, 2012. http://evolutionarypsychiatry.blogspot.com.
74. Michael Ellsberg, "How I Overcame Bipolar II (and Saved My Own Life)," *Forbes*, July 18, 2011. www.forbes.com.
75. Ellsberg, "How I Overcame Bipolar II (and Saved My Own Life)."
76. Quoted in University of Michigan, "Do Drugs for Bipolar Disorder 'Normalize' Brain Gene Function? U-M Study Suggests So," April 11, 2013. www.uofmhealth.org.
77. National Alliance on Mental Illness, "Bipolar Disorder."

List of Illustrations

Index

Note: Boldface page numbers indicate illustrations.

Index

About the Author

Peggy J. Parks holds a bachelor of science degree from Aquinas College in Grand Rapids, Michigan, where she graduated magna cum laude. An author who has written more than a hundred educational books on a wide variety of topics, Parks lives in Muskegon, Michigan, a town that she says inspires her writing because of its location on the shores of Lake Michigan.

About the Author